Edward I

A Captivating Guide to the Life and Death of the Hammer of the Scots and His Impact on the History of England

Free Bonus from Captivating History (Available for a Limited time)

Hi History Lovers!

Now you have a chance to join our exclusive history list so you can get your first history ebook for free as well as discounts and a potential to get more history books for free! Simply visit the link below to join.

Captivatinghistory.com/ebook

Also, make sure to follow us on Facebook, Twitter and Youtube by searching for Captivating History.

Table of Contents

Introduction: England's First Real King

Although there were, of course, kings in Britain prior to King Edward, in many ways he is viewed as a crucial starting point in English history. He proved himself to be a powerful monarch early on and worked tirelessly to consolidate his gains. He was a stern ruler but farsighted enough to realize his kingdom would have greater stability if the majority of his subjects were well cared for and (at least to some degree) happy.

This authoritarian monarch made great strides in England's march toward a more constitutional monarchy by allowing reforms that gave the people of England more control over their own destinies. Edward—the son of the rather weak and ineffectual King Henry III—sought an orderly path forward for England. He also sought to distance himself from the perceived failures of his father.

Edward's predecessor was known primarily for corruption and giving in to the whims of his own personal cronies in the royal court. He was especially criticized for showering favors upon his wife's family members. These actions not only led to great resentment but actual bloodshed, as factions formed and revolts were waged. When Edward came to the throne, he wished to distance himself from all of this unnecessary and dangerous personal intrigue. Edward did not want to concern himself with the trifling affairs of the royal court.

For him, the establishment and consolidation of his own royal authority trumped everything else. He would spend his entire life expanding the borders of his domain, establishing a legacy that carries on to this day. After all, it was Edward who defeated the Welsh and instituted the title of "Prince of Wales," which a certain Prince Charles (perhaps future King Charles?) currently holds today. Yes, in many ways, the history of Britain begins with this larger-than-life monarch, King Edward. And now that you know all of that, here's the rest of his story.

Chapter 1: The King with the Long Shanks

King Edward began life on June 18ᵗʰ, 1239. He was the son of King Henry III and his wife, Queen Eleanor of Provence. His parents had a loving relationship, but it was full of drama and intrigue from the start. Much of this drama stemmed from the fact that Eleanor was not of English heritage but hailed from Provence, which is now part of modern-day France.

English court officials developed an entirely unfounded belief that she was bringing undue foreign influence into English affairs. There was also criticism early on that she was unable to produce children simply because it took her a few years to get pregnant after marrying Henry III. It was a matter of continued gossip and, yes, even concern. After all, for a monarch, having an heir meant everything, so it's fair to say that many were concerned with whether or not the new queen would be able to provide one.

At any rate, Eleanor finally put an end to the speculation by giving birth to little Edward in 1239. His birth was heralded with great fanfare, and feasts were held in his honor at the Palace of Westminster.

Although the child was just as much an heir to the Norman Conquest as he was the heir to the English crown, his father and mother decided to give him an anglicized moniker in honor of

Edward the Confessor. These parents no doubt wanted their son to grow up brave and strong just like his namesake, but Edward was a frail and often sickly child.

In the year 1246, for example, when he was just seven years of age, he became deathly ill. His parents must have wondered if their child would even get the chance to grow up at all. Edward was able to recover, and he certainly grew. Nicknamed "Longshanks" or as it would be rendered today "long shins," this small child would ultimately grow into a strapping young man and reach over six feet in height. Since the average height in those days was much shorter, he was considered quite tall by his contemporaries.

In 1247, King Henry III granted his son the great honor of being able to go on official hunts in Windsor Forest. Such hunts were not just about bagging game for the many feasts in the castle; it was also a form of great sport. On these hunts, Edward was able to learn how to handle knives and swords and was given a crash course in archery.

These skills were good for hunting beasts, but the hunts and training also impressed upon the young prince the important role that warfare would play in his future. War with France, in particular, would become increasingly likely. Ancestors of the English kings had come from Normandy, a region that is today part of mainland France. Back in the 13th century, however, England had lost control of much of its French territory, and by the 1250s, King Henry III was only in control of the southwestern region, of what was called Gascony, otherwise known as Aquitaine to the English.

This last foothold in France was essentially considered a crown jewel, and it was vigorously safeguarded. In fact, Henry III had chosen a wife from the French region of Provence partially in an effort to help bolster his claims in southern France. Henry very much hoped that he could regain lost ground in France, including the region from which his wife came. But Gascony was the prized treasure, and it was the region that Edward would hopefully rule one day as a duchy.

In September 1249, these aspirations were made official when King Henry III officially granted his son the Duchy of Gascony. Barely six months later, a series of revolts broke out in Gascony, putting Edward's claims over the region in peril. The man in charge of Gascony's affairs was Royal Lieutenant Simon de Montfort.

Montfort was actually the king's brother-in-law, and he was known as a hero of the Crusades. He was a fiery character. His no-holds-bar methodology gained him praise during the Crusades, but it only seemed to cause more problems in Gascony. Montfort attempted to crush the revolts under his iron fist, which caused the rebels to revolt even more vigorously. And soon enough, the whole country would go up in flames, with nonstop fighting that rendered any true sense of English authority unfeasible.

Initially, King Henry III backed Montfort to the hilt, sending regular funds and troops to help boost his efforts. But by 1251, King Henry was largely dissatisfied with how things were playing out and began to slowly pull back his support. Things then came to a head on Christmas Day of 1251. The two men met face to face and began berating each other. It's pretty bold to berate a king, but then again, Montfort, the legendary veteran of the Crusades, was about as bold as they came.

The king could have had Montfort's head for his insolence but instead simply ordered that Montfort be stripped of authority in Gascony. Montfort then sought refuge in France proper. Even so, he refused to abide by this ruling. In complete and utter revolt against the king himself, Montfort landed in Gascony and began fanning the fires of dissension even further with his antics.

This further destabilization led King Henry III to consider direct military intervention. The trouble was the king was strapped for cash at the time, and empty royal coffers are not very conducive to funding wars abroad. The only way to raise funds was to enforce a highly unpopular tax on the population. But Henry III knew he couldn't do so in an arbitrary fashion. So, instead of issuing an ultimatum, he convened a meeting of local leaders from all of the English counties. This assembly was called a "parlement," and it was a forerunner to the parliamentarian government of modern England. These gathered notables immediately rendered pushback to the king's desire to fund a war in Gascony.

The king tried a more political tact in 1252 by having his thirteen-year-old son Edward participate in a public ceremony in which his grant in Gascony was officially renewed. Local Gascons were in attendance, and despite the turmoil in their native region, they rendered homage to Edward. This was all for show, as it was a non-military effort to bolster royal claims to Gascony.

The situation in Gascony would become even more unstable in the meantime. In early 1253, the Spanish region of Castile, which neighbored Gascony, expressed support for the rebels. Castile was the greatest and most powerful region of Spain at the time, and it had a rather audacious character named Alfonso X rise to the throne.

Alfonso knew that if he backed the rebels, he had a chance of incorporating Gascony into his own kingdom. So that's what he did. And soon, he was not only tacitly supporting the rebels but also amassing his own troops on Gascony's border. This series of events finally forced King Henry III to act. He amassed what forces he could and landed them in Gascony. The teenage Edward was left at home with his mother acting as regent.

Henry's troops were ultimately successful in their bid to put down the rebels, and Castile's king, Alfonso, was brought to the table for negotiations. Interestingly enough, the terms were quite simple. Alfonso declared his willingness to cease aiding the rebels and forego any territorial claims over Gascony if he was provided with a suitable marriage alliance.

Royal heads of state often married other royals to forge strategic alliances. And Alfonso's declaration of his desire to enter into one was largely an act of good faith since it showed his interest to develop closer ties to England. But he was not calling for himself to be a member of this alliance. On the contrary, his idea was to have his sister Eleanor wed England's Prince Edward.

Alfonso also stipulated that Edward be given significant land endowments, including endowments in Gascony. They say that "all's fair in love and war," and it seemed that if the crafty king of Castile could not get Gascony through war, he would attempt to get it through love. Alfonso also wanted to meet the prince for himself prior to the union and declared his desire to knight him.

As such, on May 29th, of that fateful year of 1253, fifteen-year-old Prince Edward and his mother sailed to Gascony. His father was mopping up the last pockets of rebel resistance, and Edward was provided with the opportunity to head to the front lines to see the troops in action. The main event, of course, was Edward's impending wedding to Eleanor. And although this was an arranged marriage, Edward took strides to indicate that he was a full partner in the decision.

In the draft of the marriage agreement, Edward stated that he had "willingly and spontaneously" decided to marry Eleanor. He also added, for the record, that she was an ideal bride "whose prudence and beauty we have heard by general report." It was indeed a marriage of convenience, but Edward wished to indicate that it was agreeable enough for him regardless.

Upon Edward's arrival, he ended up staying in Bordeaux until September. He went off alone to Spain, while his parents, the reigning king and queen, returned to England. It was a big deal for the prince to travel without his parents, as it showed a great deal of trust had been given to him. Even so, he was still surrounded by a good chunk of the royal court as his official entourage.

On October 18th, 1253, Prince Edward and company found themselves in Burgos—a traditional mainstay for royalty in Castile. The records go dark on what might have transpired during this visit, but historians believe that Edward was likely knighted around November 1st at the Las Huelgas monastery. And shortly thereafter, Edward married his bride, Eleanor.

After a brief honeymoon, Edward and his wife headed off to Gascony, where they arrived on November 21st. Edward was now in charge of his own duchy. It was a great boost to young Edward's pride, but it wasn't long before he had to take a good hard look at just how desperate the state of his new duchy was. Gascony had been devastated by war, and its coffers were bare.

As such, it wasn't long before Edward had to tax his new subjects to fill the treasury. The residents of Gascony did not approve, and new revolts began to break out. In early 1255, Edward led troops to quash the rebel offensive. Fortresses and even whole cities had to be girded against the threat of this onslaught. Edward also had to construct naval craft. All of this, of course, required money.

In the meantime, King Henry III was in England. He found himself putting the kibosh on a tournament he was hosting in order to send knights to aid his son's dilemma in Gascony. The reinforcements must have helped since Edward ended the revolt and restored order to his duchy. Sixteen-year-old Edward was now the master of his own domain, and standing at a whopping six feet tall, he had indeed lived up to his nickname as the King with the Long Shanks.

Chapter 2 – Ready to Be King in His Own Right

"Perhaps everyone should have a crown."

-King Edward I

Soon after Prince Edward's royal marriage and his acquisition of Gascony, he was itching to get out on his own, even though his father worried that his son was about to slide into all-out rebellion. King Henry III, on at least one occasion, is said to have questioned his son about his loyalty to his face. Edward was not about to openly defy his father, though, and ultimately acquiesced to the wishes of the sitting king.

Even so, Edward took pains to make himself a more formidable leader in Gascony, increasing the size of his own personal guard. He was often accompanied by no less than two hundred horsemen. On his seventeenth birthday in June of 1256, Edward engaged in his first royal games. Here, just as he had in his youth during royal hunts, he could truly prove his mettle as a military leader.

These early royal games—sometimes dubbed "tournaments"—were often orchestrated as nothing short of make-believe shows of military might. There was a bit of pomp and circumstance involved, but the practicality of allowing the king's men to practice what they would actually do in battle was of extreme importance. These tournaments often boasted two teams that would face off against each other, imitating an actual battlefield engagement between two opposing armies.

The participants all wore protective armor and utilized blunted weapons to minimize casualties, but the fact that grown men were knocking each other off horses with the equivalent of metal clubs still made it dangerous. According to court chronicler Matthew Paris, many were badly injured during the course of these exercises, and more than a few perished.

Shortly after these royal exercises of martial might came to a close, Prince Edward went north to take a tour of Scotland. In those days, Scotland was not yet a part of the English domain. But it was a closely tied neighbor and an important place for any budding English monarch to visit. Edward also had to acquaint himself with the dynastic ties between the two realms within his own family.

Just a few years prior, Edward's little sister, Margaret, had been duly wed to Alexander III, King of the Scots. Edward's visit to Scotland lasted for about three weeks, and not very much is known of what happened. At any rate, Edward was soon back in Gascony, where tensions between his leadership style and the overriding authority of his father remained high. Edward also began to engage in reckless and excessive behavior that at times needed to be reined in by his dad.

More problems presented themselves in Wales with the rise of the Welsh leader Llywelyn ap Gruffudd. Henry III turned to Edward to lead an expedition against the Welsh upstart. According to English chronicler Matthew Paris, it was something that Edward himself perceived as a great opportunity to flex his muscles. Or, as Paris put it, "Edward was determined to check the impetuous rashness of the Welsh, to punish their presumption, and to wage war against them to their extermination."

However, although Edward was zealous in his mission, the terrible weather in the region caused the entire expedition to stall. Paris informs us, "The whole winter that year was so wet and stormy that the entire country of Wales was utterly inaccessible to the English, and thus Edward's labour and expenditure of money were fruitless and of no avail." Wales is indeed known for its unpredictable and harsh weather, and it seems that the very elements of Wales were its best defense, at least in regards to this ill-fated attempt to subjugate its people.

And while the weather kept Edward's forces at bay, he had other pressing problems, namely time and money. The longer things were delayed, the more money was wasted, and the less money he had, the less successful his efforts to fund the war would be. This difficult situation led Edward to reach out to his dear old uncle, Richard Cornwall. When this proved unfruitful, he finally swallowed his pride and begged his father for a loan.

But King Henry III was too preoccupied with his own problems to be of much help. The king, like usual, was cash-strapped and unable to raise proper funds for the war effort. In addition to this, Henry was also quite determined to turn the whole affair into a kind of teaching moment, one in which Edward would have to figure out how to resolve the problem in Wales on his own. During one of their exchanges over the matter, King Henry is said to have suddenly snapped "What is it to me?" before declaring, "The land is yours by my gift. I am concerned with other business." Thus, if Edward wanted to one day rule England and be the big shot who controlled outlying territory such as Wales, he would have to figure out how to develop his own strategies.

As Edward's efforts in Wales stalled, Llywelyn was busy consolidating his own power base, bringing all of the local Welsh nobles to the forefront. He partially did so by promising them land for their allegiance to his cause. One Welsh witness to these events later recorded them for posterity, saying, "[Llywelyn kept] nothing for himself but fame and honor."

Llywelyn was willing to reward those who struggled against England by giving them their own landed estates in Wales. All he wanted in return was to be recognized as the great Welsh leader who enabled them to defy the English crown. He had kept the English at bay in the north of the country, and now, Llywelyn and those loyal to him were heading farther southward. Soon enough, the Welsh warriors were even striking at English settlements in the Welsh and English borderlands.

This finally brought the fight to Edward, who had been strengthening his forces around fortresses positioned outside the towns of Cardigan and Carmarthen. While most outside of Britain likely associate "Cardigan" with cardigan sweaters rather than siege warfare, this town would come to play a pivotal role in Edward's clash with Llywelyn. Even though Llywelyn could have this English stronghold veritably surrounded on land since it was nestled on the Welsh coast, it could still have crucial aid shipped to it from English holdings in nearby Ireland.

Edward sent his troops from nearby Carmarthen to break the land siege that was taking place at Cardigan. However, as soon as they left Carmarthen, they were intercepted by Llywelyn Ap Gruffudd's forces. On June 2nd, 1257, Edward's forces fought with Llewelyn's men in open battle. The results were not good for Edward, as his army was decimated.

In fact, the situation was so bad that King Henry III was finally forced to get involved. He rallied more troops around the town of Chester that August and then had this contingent join what was left of Edward's forces to march on the Welsh warriors together. Henry's army did well enough at first, but it quickly became bogged down in Wales. His men ultimately had to retreat back to Chester, getting ambushed by Welsh fighters along the way.

This abortive attempt to bring Llywelyn to task had emboldened him more than ever before. He was now the undisputed champion of the Welsh, who had not only dared to stand up to the English but also had successfully beaten back their strongest armies. Other Welsh warlords who might have previously been skeptical of Llywelyn's leadership were more firmly in his corner. With this new clout at his disposal, Llywelyn was insisting that he be officially hailed as the "Prince of Wales" in early 1258.

Edward found himself losing faith in his own mother and father. Not only had King Henry III failed to provide funds for his military campaigns, but even his father's own forces were not enough to defeat the so-called Prince of Wales, Llywelyn ap

Gruffudd.

And on top of this, a familial struggle of another sort had been playing out. This struggle involved Edward's mom's side of the family—the Savoyards—and his father's relatives—the Lusignans. By 1257, Edward had fallen in with the Lusignan crowd, and the Savoyards did not like it. Edward was particularly frustrated with his mother or rather her family because her kin had been in charge of the estates in Wales that Llywelyn had seized. Edward once again moved closer to his Lusignan relatives, in particular his uncles William and Aymer de Valence.

This was of grave concern to Edward's mother and the whole Savoyard faction. If Edward fell in with the Lusignans, their own power base would be significantly undermined in favor of the Lusignan family. And if they were not already worried enough, on April 1st, 1258, members of the Lusignan faction and the Savoyard faction literally came to blows when Aymer de Valence had a group of thugs under his command ransack the grounds of Queen Eleanor's adviser. In the melee, one of those charged with guarding the premises was killed.

The Savoyards were immediately outraged. By the end of the month, they had cobbled together a large assembly of knights and had them convene at the Great Hall of the Palace of Westminster to personally request the king to push back against the Lusignans. Presented with such a formidable group, King Henry III was momentarily convinced to agree with them. But as soon as the powerful assembly left, the king reversed course and built up his own large army.

That May, a group of nobles, including the once-spurned Simon de Montfort, convened and called for reforms. They drafted the Provisions of Oxford, which called for limits to be placed on the Lusignans. This was done through the transfer of royal castles that had been under the dominion of the king's cronies (largely the Lusignans). These castles went to approved English earls instead.

Edward initially resisted this movement and even defied the reformers by appointing Lusignan relatives to important posts. He made Guy de Lusignan in charge of the Island of Oléron, which was just off the shores of Gascony. Edward made another Lusignan relative—Geoffrey de Lusignan—the chief administrator of Gascony itself.

Despite this show of defiance, once the Lusignans' power and sway began to recede, Edward switched sides. His Lusignan relatives left their posts in government and were forced into exile. The fact that this council or proto-parliament of nobles was able to force the hands of both King Henry III and his son Edward was monumental in the push toward limiting the English crown's absolute authority. Although the executive power of the royal monarch would ebb and flow over the following centuries, this watershed moment would stand out as an example. Royal authority could indeed be curtailed if a concerted effort was made.

Along with bringing the Lusignans to heel, the council also managed to conclude a ceasefire of sorts with the aggressive Prince of Wales, Llywelyn ap Gruffudd. However, it didn't last long, and by the following fall, fighting had erupted in the Welsh borderlands once again. Under the pretext of aiding the struggle against Gruffudd, Edward made his way back to England. Once there, he engaged in three separate tournaments, which, all fun aside, were essentially a means to recruit able young men and drill them into fighting shape.

Edward seemed to have accepted the wishes of the parliamentary council. In the midst of his jousting at the tournaments, Edward fired off a letter to a chief official in Chester, in which he seemingly agreed that the council's will was just. In the letter, which dates back to August 21st, 1259, Edward states, "If common justice is denied to any one of our subjects by us or our bailiffs, we lose the favor of God and man, and our lordship is belittled." But as much of an idealist as Edward might have presented himself in this note, there were certainly ulterior motives behind his sudden support of the reformers.

His old associate Montfort was a member of the council, and Edward and Montfort had come to a quiet little agreement with each other, in which Edward would support him in the "settlement of his personal claims." In return, Montfort would pledge his support for Edward via his position on the council. In the fall of 1259, this solidarity was first displayed. Both Edward and Montfort opposed King Henry III's recent treaty with France, which formally gave up any remaining claims to the long-lost lands of Normandy, Anjou, Poitou, and Maine in exchange for French acknowledgment of English sovereignty over Gascony.

Many viewed the treaty to be perfectly pragmatic and sensible. It simply gave up claims that had lost any real force long ago in exchange for formal French recognition of the real English prize—Gascony. For most, this treaty made complete sense. Yet, here were Edward and Montfort, both expressing their displeasure with the deal. Nevertheless, King Henry III and his entourage sailed the English Channel to meet with the king of France. On December 4th, the Treaty of Paris was signed, sealing the deal brokered between the two monarchs.

While Henry III and much of his court were away in France, Edward saw a chance to exert more authority in England. Just about as soon as his father's back was turned, he fired administrators of his fortresses whom his father had appointed and replaced them with his own handpicked officials. Edward also managed to install himself in Bristol Castle, making it essentially his headquarters in England.

Edward then found another point of contention to set himself at odds with his father. According to the Provisions of Oxford, the council was supposed to meet three times a year. While Henry was abroad in France, the council was once again scheduled to convene. This presented a problem because the council had to decide whether to postpone the meeting until the king returned. Henry had already expressly forbidden any meetings in his absence. Nevertheless, not missing an opportunity, Prince Edward supported the view that the council should convene regardless.

In April of 1260, tensions became so extreme that King Henry III was wondering if his own son might be plotting a coup. It was only through the mediation of Edward's uncle, the Earl of Cornwall, that the mounting crisis was averted. King Henry III mostly blamed Montfort for influencing his son's actions, so he was able to let bygones be bygones. But Montfort did not receive the same treatment. He was put on trial for his actions.

In the lead-up to Montfort's trial, the so-called Prince of Wales—Llywelyn ap Gruffudd—began to stir things up in the Welsh borderlands once again. Soon, his forces were laying siege to the English outpost of Builth. The fortress held out for a few months, but then right in the midst of Montfort's trial, its defenders were overrun and the fortifications destroyed.

King Henry was shocked at the news but was unsure of how to approach the situation. His advisers were equally perplexed, with some urging restraint while others suggested that an immediate military offensive was necessary. Edward was one of those pressing for a military response. This was due, in no small part, to the fact that Builth was one of the castles that were supposed to be under his administration. But even as the drumbeat for war against Wales seemed to be growing louder, on September 1st, 1260, right at the eleventh hour, a peace treaty was brokered that called for a ceasefire for at least two years.

Due to the disturbance in Wales, the efforts to bring Montfort to trial were entirely derailed. And Montfort himself returned to England on April 25th, 1262, and began to stir up trouble for King Henry III. Soon, he was gathering a force of rebels at the town of Oxford—the very site where the provisions to reform the monarchy had been established. Montfort unleashed his forces that June on the properties that had been under the queen of England's and her followers' control.

It was a scorched-earth affair, with Montfort and company destroying not only fortifications but also farms, gardens, and even the hovels of the average citizenry that just happened to be nearby. Even worse, in one instance, a cathedral was ransacked, and the bishop was seized and taken as a hostage.

Edward was initially on the sidelines during this conflict, but after he realized what an end to his father's royal power would mean for him, he immediately dropped what he was doing in Wales and headed off to aid his family. Edward arrived in London and found that his parents were holed up in the Tower of London, apparently ready to make one final stand should Montfort's forces march against them.

At that point, Montfort was doing everything he could to turn city officials in London against the monarchy. He issued a challenge to city leaders, saying they were either for or against the Provisions of Oxford. The pressured city officials wished to show their support for the provisions and sent a delegation to the king, who was still holed up in the Tower of London, urging him to do the same.

Edward was galvanized to take action. On June 29th, he and his supporters headed over to the so-called "New Temple" fortification, which had once been the headquarters of the Knights Templar. This complex had also served as a kind of unofficial money depository, where affluent nobles had placed their treasures for safekeeping. Edward found the place locked up tight once he arrived.

In order to get the keys, he actually told those in charge that he was there to take a look at his mother's jewels. It sounds somewhat ridiculous to have Edward speaking of how he just wanted to take a peek at his mom's old jewelry, but this is apparently what he did. And it apparently worked. The guardians of the temple fell for the ruse and opened the place right up for Edward. As soon as Edward and his gang had access, they wasted no time ransacking the place. They tore through the hoard of wealth stored there, busted open safes, and smashed any other barrier in their way, pocketing as much loot as they possibly could.

It seems Edward was sick and tired of his father's legacy. His father was often too broke to fund his own military campaigns. So, Edward quite literally took matters into his own hands by seizing wealth for himself so that he could finance what would become a personal war with Montfort. However, his actions would not go without consequences. Those who were on the sidelines as to whether or not they should support the king obviously would not take too kindly to having their life's savings confiscated from them. And soon after this unilateral raid on the temple, many more had been galvanized to join the revolt against King Henry III.

In the meantime, Montfort was on the move, attempting to seize what fortifications he could. Most importantly, he had taken control of Kent and many important ports. By July 4th, 1262,

King Henry III, a veritable prisoner in the Tower of London, was finally forced to agree to the terms laid out by the angry mob outside.

His wife had made a daring escape from the Tower by boarding a boat perched on the Thames River. She headed off to Windsor, where she hoped to seek refuge. However, she was intercepted on the way there when the boat passed under London Bridge. Here, she was pelted with not only shouts and curses but also stones, rotten eggs, and other pieces of garbage. The ship's captain was able to get the queen to safety, but the boat had to be diverted to the bishop of London's palace.

When Edward heard of the abuse that his mother had suffered, he became determined to fully support his parents and dedicated himself to the destruction of Montfort once and for all. Nevertheless, Montfort was well ahead of Edward and his marauding band of fighters. He entered London two days ahead of Edward. This led to the king and queen's direct surrender. This meant that Edward and his band of fighters were now on their own.

Chapter 3 – Taking Back the Kingdom

"I am Henry of Winchester—your king! Do not kill me!"

-King Henry III

With his father locked up in the Tower of London and his kingdom overrun by his uncle Montfort, Prince Edward was like a king in waiting, as he was at risk of no longer having a kingdom to call his own. As Edward roved about the countryside with his band of loyal knights, Montfort sought to consolidate his control. In the middle of October 1262, a new parliament convened in Westminster. Montfort and his cohorts were in attendance.

It was at this moment that Edward decided to strike, and not just militarily but through intrigue as well. Behind the scenes, Edward had already laid the groundwork to gain the upper hand by promising nobles that had sided with Montfort that if they switched back to the royal cause, they would be rewarded with landed estates. This was apparently enough to convince many to join sides with Edward.

So, by the time parliament convened, Montfort, who thought he had the situation under control, was in for a surprise. Edward's new supporters forged an army and quickly regained control of Oxford, which was followed by Winchester. That December, they were already on the verge of taking Dover and London. This stunning reversal caused Montfort to think twice and seek negotiations rather than pursue further fighting. He even demanded that a truce be mediated by the king of France. This request was obliged, and Henry and Edward went across the English Channel to France, where they argued their points. The French king at this point—perhaps due to Henry's pragmatic Treaty of Paris—was firmly in the king's corner. This left Montfort no choice but to continue a losing war against the resurgent royalist party.

Shortly after Montfort's return to England, he reignited his war against the royalists. The royalist faction struck a decisive blow against Montfort's forces on April 5th, 1263, during a battle at Northampton. Here, in a single engagement, about eighty of Montfort's knights, along with his own son—Simon—were seized and taken as prisoners of war. The bitter fighting would continue for several months. By the spring of 1264, Montfort was holed up in London with what remained of his forces.

That May, the royalist troops came marching up from the south, planning to lay siege to what remained of Montfort's once-formidable rebellion. However, at this point, some overtures toward negotiations were made, and King Henry III urged restraint. But the young and incensed Edward insisted that there should be no quarter for the rebels. On May 13th, in answer to some of the entreaties being made by Montfort's faction, Edward fired off a missive that read, in part, "From this time forth we will do our utmost to inflict injury upon your persons and possessions."

Edward did not care what kind of excuses were made; he was now ready to utterly destroy the opposition. In the final battle between the two factions, the royalists had a robust army made up of three divisions. Henry III led the division on the left, Richard of Cornwall rode in front of the division in the center, and Edward charged ahead of the knights that made up the right flank.

This engagement would become known as the Battle of Lewes, and things did not turn out so well for the royalists. Richard of Cornwall's troops were smashed, and he was taken prisoner.

Henry was forced to flee after his division took a beating. Edward's forces fared a little better but were still forced to retreat from the field of battle when Edward, in his zeal, gave chase to a withdrawing contingent of Montfort's regiment. Upon his return, he and his troops realized the rest of the royalists had been broken.

Edward regrouped with what remained of Henry's entourage, and this combined group holed themselves up in the priory of Lewes. Montfort could have stormed this last refuge but did not; he knew the political implications would have been too dire. He was a diehard Crusader, known for giving his life for the cause of Christendom. And in the medieval mindset, storming a church to kill a monarch would have tarnished that image.

Instead, Montfort was content to consider the king and his son, Edward, his prisoners. Montfort's victory was a great boon for him and his followers. Even though they were surrounded and greatly outnumbered, they managed to overcome what had initially appeared to be insurmountable odds. But this struggle was far from over. Montfort, more than anyone else, knew that as long as King Henry and his son were still alive, he could not claim the kingship for himself.

And Henry and Edward still had one ace up their sleeve—the queen. Queen Eleanor of Provence was still at large, just across the English Channel in mainland France, and she was most certainly not being idle. She had already galvanized a large contingent of troops and supporters that consisted of royalist exiles. She forged a veritable army complete with naval support, and they fully intended to take back King Henry III's kingdom.

However, by November, Eleanor's efforts had petered out, and the proposed invasion was put on the shelf. In May 1265, help came from an unexpected source. The earl of Gloucester—Gilbert de Clare—was apparently determined to do what he could to restore the monarchy. Gilbert had initially supported Montfort, but after victory was at hand and spoils distributed, Gilbert ended up feeling slighted by Montfort.

Unbeknownst to Montfort, Gilbert quietly switched sides and came out in support of the royalists. Before openly opposing

Montfort, Gilbert worked a bit of subterfuge by pressuring Montfort to allow Edward to have some liberties. It is perhaps a bit hard to fathom why Montfort would allow a person so dangerous to his own ambition their freedom, but he ultimately obliged the powerful and influential earl of Gloucester this request.

Although Edward was still watched by armed men, he would no longer be locked in a cell. Edward managed to break free of all surveillance on May 28th, 1265, under the ruse of wishing to ride out to the country "to exercise [his] horses." It seems quite incredible that Edward was given the opportunity to ride so far from Montfort's grasp. However, it must be said that Montfort did take some precautions by having a few guards on horseback join Edward.

Edward had a trick up his sleeve. He specifically ran every single horse to exhaustion except for one. And as soon as they were far enough out of range, Edward jumped on this fresh and spry horse. He rode off at full speed, shouting back at his captors who sat on their exhausted mounts, "Lordings, I bid you good day! Greet my father well, and tell him I hope to see him soon, to release him from custody!"

And sure enough, Edward kept right on riding, galloping all the way out to Ludlow where Gilbert de Clare, Earl of Gloucester, was waiting for them. Edward then joined him in what would become the latest round of warfare waged against Montfort. There were some early gains for Edward, such as the taking of Worcester and other strategic fortifications.

The seizure of Worcester, in particular, caught the defenders off-guard. Montfort's own son Simon, who was supposed to be leading the defense, was literally caught sleeping. Simon just barely escaped with his life by sneaking off the battlements at the very last minute. He hopped in a boat and rowed with all his might to the other side of the castle's moat.

In medieval times, a renowned man's castle was often his house. So, there was perhaps nothing more inglorious than someone like Simon having to flee his own castle, row across his own moat, and then run from the scene of battle just to save his own life.

In the meantime, Montfort made a deal with the ever-ambitious Llywelyn of Wales. This led to a combined Montfortian and Welsh force colliding with the forces of the earl of Gloucester and Prince Edward. On August 4th, 1265, during what would later be dubbed the Second Barons' War, these two sides duked it out at Evesham. At this point, Montfort's forces had been cornered at Evesham, which was situated within a loop of the River Avon. Surrounded by water on three sides and the forces of his enemies on the other, Montfort was forced to make a final stand.

Montfort really didn't stand much of a chance. His forces were easily overwhelmed by the larger army, and since they were unable to effectively maneuver, they were quickly hacked to pieces. Although Edward had been spared from execution by his enemies in the past, he once again indicated that there should be "no quarter" given to his own enemies. As such, all of Montfort's men were systematically decimated as they frantically fought what was, for them, clearly a losing battle.

In the midst of this slaughter, Montfort was seized by Edward's pre-selected "death squad." Edward had apparently created a special task force made up of some of his deadliest knights with the sole duty of hunting down Montfort and delivering the final blow. Montfort died after a lance was hurled through his throat. This was enough to kill him, but as soon as his body hit the ground, more of Edward's warriors joined in, chopping at the slain commander until his head, hands, and feet were severed from his body. As a final insult, they chopped off Montfort's penis. The frenzied assailants then proceeded to shove it into Montfort's mouth.

In the melee, King Henry, who was present under the watch of Montfort, was nearly killed by the royalists until his shouts of, "I am Henry of Winchester—your king! Do not kill me!" were heard. After the warriors were restrained, Prince Edward escorted his dad to safety, away from the complete and utter carnage. It was a terrible, bloody scene. But nevertheless, the kingdom had been reclaimed, and the struggle against Montfort had finally come to an end.

Chapter 4 – A Lasting Peace and the Need for a Crusade

"We shall then defeat the whole lot of them in one go!"

-King Edward I

An inordinate number of lives were lost at the notorious Battle of Evesham. Edward's victory was indeed complete since his principal foe, Simon de Montfort, had finally been put down for good. Edward's success in battle had restored his father to the throne and bolstered his own image as the heir apparent. It would be a long time before anyone would dare to question the English monarchy's authority again. The monarchy had political capital as it were, and they were ready to spend it.

Despite the bloodshed, Edward was willing to show some degree of mercy. When some former supporters approached Edward, suing for peace, he gladly gave it, promising that their professed allegiance to him was enough to ensure their safety. Their property was not ensured, though. In the fall of 1265, King Henry III announced at a parliamentary meeting in Winchester that any territory seized by the king's faithful subjects did not have to be restored to the Montfortian rebels.

Edward's own uncle, Richard of Cornwall, was appalled at this measure. He felt that it would lead to a renewed cycle of violence.

If the rebels were not reintegrated back into society by having their property restored, he reasoned that it would only be a matter of time before these disgruntled disinherited individuals began saber-rattling against the king again.

In London, the seizure of property was a major issue, with many of the Londoners who had sided with Montfort finding themselves ousted from their lands, while King Henry and Prince Edward rewarded those loyal to them with the seized properties. It was perhaps Edward's little brother Edmund who received the greatest boon of all, for he was given not only Montfort's own estate but also Montfort's former title as earl.

Montfort's wife, Eleanor de Montfort, King Henry III's own sister, was ferried across the English Channel and forced into exile. Her son, Simon, was also exiled once he had been captured. It is hard to imagine how this widow spent the rest of her life, as she had to live knowing how her brother and nephew had viciously brutalized her husband.

At any rate, on October 29th, 1265, Henry III's wife returned from her own exile in France, meeting Edward at the port of Dover. Edward then shepherded his returned mother to his father. The royal couple was finally reunited after nearly two years of being apart. Edward had also been reunited with his own wife, Eleanor of Castile, who at that time was pregnant with her and Edward's child.

As events continued to progress, it seems that Richard of Cornwall was right in his estimation that the king was sowing further bitterness and harvesting more potential enemies through his lack of mercy and reconciliation. Soon, pockets of rebellion began to emerge. During the ensuing campaigns, Edward once again led an army, taking part in the siege of the Cinque Ports situated around Kent, Sussex, and Essex in March 1266. These ports had become a refuge for Montfort sympathizers and essentially became a nest of pirates. In order to have continued peace in the kingdom, these valuable ports needed to be secured.

Along with bringing overwhelming force to the table, Edward switched tactics and offered more conciliatory terms of peace. He let it be known that those who laid down their arms would be given their freedom, their property, and a full pardon for past allegiances. Edward's merciful stance was indeed appealing, and the tired and weary rebels gladly gave up their arms.

However, the following month of April brought renewed violence from those who did not end up quite as fortunate as those at the Cinque Ports. The rebels who did not receive their land back had all the reason in the world to continue to wage a guerilla war. And that is precisely what they did. They began to systematically raid counties in East Anglia, the Midlands, and Hampshire. By May, the king's forces had struck back and successfully quashed rebellions in Derbyshire and Chesterfield. Edward battled it out with rebels in Hampshire in an intense engagement that actually saw the prince in hand-to-hand combat with the rebels' leader.

The next major bastion of resistance the royal forces put down was Montfort's old stronghold of Kenilworth Castle. This region and the castle were now considered the property of Edward's little brother, Edmund. Edmund led the charge against the rebels that summer.

In the midst of all this, Edward's wife, Eleanor of Castile, successfully gave birth to a baby boy on July 14th, 1266. The child was named John in honor of Edward's grandfather.

This child was born into a kingdom in turmoil. Despite several successes, the insurgency continued unabated. Edward increasingly came to realize that an amicable agreement must be presented to the opposition. The fighting between the rebels and the royalists only came to a close with the Dictum of Kenilworth.

The arrangement stipulated that the rebels' estates could be returned to them as long as they paid a fine. This fine would compensate the royalists who had seized the rebels' land. It wasn't the best of terms for the rebels, but it was indeed a path forward. Although the rebels were burdened by a fine, they had the opportunity to reclaim some of their property. And the royalists who had previously been promised land were compensated for their losses as well.

Even so, not everyone was happy. As the fateful year of 1267 came around, new problems emerged on the nearby island fortress of Ely, where the so-called "disinherited" were calling for more to be done to alleviate their burden. King Henry III sent a message to these rabble-rousers, declaring that he would be fully justified to keep their land without any opportunity of recovery. In response, the disgruntled rebels of Ely declared that their having to pay "redemption dues" was akin to a permanent disinheritance.

Henry was incensed at their obstinance and dispatched a fleet of ships to lay siege to the fortress. His fleet was swatted away by the defenders, and the royalists endured a heavy cost in terms of manpower.

It was at this point in this seemingly never-ending drama that the earl of Gloucester decided to switch sides once again and team up with the remaining rebels. This powerful earl gathered together yet another formidable army in April 1267 and positioned them in London.

England seemed on the brink of civil war, but a visiting papal legate—Cardinal Ottobuono—played a pivotal and surprising role by brokering a peace deal at the very last minute, right before terrible bloodshed was about to be unleashed. This representative of the pope—a figure that all Christians looked up to back then—declared that he would institute a relief fund for the disinherited that would be backed by the clergy. This effort at appeasement calmed the situation and allowed for a rewriting of the Dictum of Kenilworth. The most important revision was the declaration that any former rebel who sought to redeem their land could regain access to it as soon as they began payments of their redemption dues rather than having to wait until after the dues were fully paid.

The idea that the disinherited would have an immediate return of their property, albeit while being forced to pay a fine, was appealing enough. This had also apparently been the earl of Gloucester's ultimatum, so once these terms were met, he agreed to put down his weapons. All that was left was for Edward's troops to put down a final batch of rebel holdouts in Ely. This group was easily quashed, and with its submission, the rebellion was finally over.

Another loose end was tied up in Wales. Later that summer, a lasting peace agreement was settled with the local potentate—Llywelyn ap Gruffudd. After several years of struggle, the heir apparent to the throne, Prince Edward, had come out on top. He was now twenty-eight years old and a veteran of epic battles and immense intrigue. But even so, his father Henry was still on the throne, so Edward was forced to play a subordinate role.

Nevertheless, there was still an opportunity for Edward to shine abroad. Edward lived during the height of the Crusades, which had the lords and nobles of Europe raising troops to march off to the Levant to either defend or reclaim Christian lands from Islamic forces.

As peace in England made Prince Edward's days more monotonous and routine, the notion of him leading an army in the Crusades became more and more appealing. King Henry III, however, was understandably concerned about such a venture. Edward was his heir apparent. Should he perish, it would be a terrible blow to England.

The pope was brought into the discussion, and in the spring of 1268, he was moved to intervene, sending a missive to Edward advising him that it would be better for him to remain behind and send his younger brother Edmund in his place. Edward wouldn't hear of it, continuing to insist that he was the best man to lead the English to the Middle East.

Eventually, Edward was able to get the papal legate, Cardinal Ottobuono, to agree with him. And King Henry III soon came around as well. It was decided that not only Edward but also his brother Edmund, as well as their cousin Henry of Almain, would all take part as commanders of a grand English Crusader force. With this matter settled, a great feast was held in honor of the would-be Crusaders on June 24th, 1268, in Northampton. It was a celebration of the Feast of St. John the Baptist as well as a going-away party for Edward and his fellow Crusaders.

Around the same time as this grand celebration, Edward's wife, Eleanor of Castile, gave birth to another son whom they named Henry in honor of Edward's father. Incredibly enough, Eleanor committed herself to joining her husband on his Crusade, even though she had recently given birth.

Of course, Eleanor would not be taking part in battle, but even the idea of her joining the entourage was considered quite bold at the time. However, the royal pair had proven themselves quite inseparable, and Eleanor was determined to undergo the rigors of the journey if it meant she could be near her husband.

Before leaving for his campaign in the Middle East, Edward was faced with a familiar problem—lack of funding. The head of this particular crusade was King Louis IX of France. King Louis was kind enough to lend Edward some of the funds needed, but the money still fell short of what was required to provide adequate arms, equipment, and rations for his troops. The most logical place to get funds was the pope. This should not have been too difficult a task since the papacy had a well-organized fundraising machine when it came to the Crusades.

However, the sitting pope had abruptly perished, throwing the cardinals in a bit of a tumult as they discussed who would next be voted in as pontiff. Unable to gain resources from the papacy, Edward had his father raise taxes on the English subjects. This was a dangerous thing to do since it was overtaxation that had prompted rebellions and revolts earlier in Henry's reign. After much discussion, in May of 1270, the parliament agreed to issue a tax as long as King Henry agreed to stand by the rights laid out in the Magna Carta. This was a declaration of rights and liberties for English subjects that had been laid out several decades prior under Edward's grandfather King John.

Sadly enough, along with reaffirming the Magna Carta, the king also agreed to issue restrictions on the local Jewish population. Jews had sought refuge in England since the days of William the Conqueror and had developed a small minority community in big English cities like London. By the 1270s, English nobles wished to curtail Jewish communities and petitioned the king to put restrictions on them.

Since King Henry was in need of cash, he agreed to do just that. In particular, he restricted moneylending, which meant that Jewish lenders could not sell the debts of those who did not pay their loans without first getting the go-ahead from the king.

After all of these matters were finally settled, Edward and his cohorts set sail from England in late August and crossed the English Channel. The group then traveled hundreds of miles overland to a prearranged rendezvous point in the region of Aigues-Mortes in southern France, arriving there in late September. But although Edward fully expected to head to the Middle East, King Louis of France had already issued a change of plans. He and the forces he led had already disembarked, not in the Middle East but in the North African city of Tunis.

Tunis was part of a larger Islamic emirate, and it was believed that if a Christian base could be planted in North Africa, Crusaders could march through Egypt and then on to the Holy Land in the Levant. Edward and company were dismayed at this change of events, but since they had traveled so far, they could hardly turn back now. As such, they also disembarked and followed the trail left by King Louis and his main contingent of Crusaders.

After some final preparations were made, Edward's army disembarked that October to join the others in North Africa. Little did he know that the mission was already a failure. King Louis had perished on August 25th, 1270, leaving the rest of the Crusaders in a state of chaos. Louis had not died in battle but had perished from an outbreak of epidemic disease, which had claimed the lives of a large chunk of his fighting force. A French knight named Charles of Anjou ultimately took control of the situation and managed to negotiate a truce with the Tunisian emir.

So, right when Edward and his men showed up at Tunis on November 9th, the hostilities had ended. They arrived just in time to see the French loading up their ships to head home to France! Edward was appalled at the incredible waste of time and energy he had just expended.

Charles of Anjou suggested that Edward and his men should set sail for Sicily to figure out what to do next. The group ended up wintering in Sicily, and by the spring, they were determined to sail eastward to the Levant. At this point in time, the Christians had lost control of much of the Holy Land but still had an outpost in the northwestern reaches of the Levant at the port city of Acre.

Edward and his cohorts reached this last outpost of Crusader might on May 9th, 1271.

It was tough times for Christian settlers in the Holy Land. The French fortress of Krak des Chevaliers had just fallen a few weeks prior to Edward's arrival. As such, the sight of Edward and his men restored some hope among the beleaguered Christians of the Levant. Perhaps the tide was about to change back in their favor.

Much of the Levant had been taken over by a sultanate that was being run by a fierce ruler by the name of Al-Malik al-Zahir Baibars." Baibars rode out to the gates of Acre to test this new arrival of Crusaders. This was not an assault but rather an intentional show of force, and Edward indeed got an eyeful. Edward had, at most, a few hundred knights at his command, and he could see thousands of fierce fighters arrayed outside the gates of Acre. After marching around the gates in full strength, Baibars ordered his troops to withdraw.

Baibars was essentially daring this fresh batch of Crusaders to come out and face him. Edward had traveled far to gain glory in combat, but he knew that facing such a large force would have been nothing short of suicidal. Nevertheless, that July, he led a contingent of knights on a raiding expedition. This was not a formal battle between armed groups but rather a punitive raid of nearby communities.

Edward's men indeed wreaked havoc, destroying farms and killing civilians in the process. These are certainly not heroic deeds. Edward's men ultimately didn't fare too well since many of them, perished from heat exhaustion, likely because they were outfitted in armor under the scorching sun.

Nevertheless, recent intrigue convinced Edward that there was still some hope of launching a major offensive. Mongol warlords had been waging war against Muslim forces northeast of the Levant, and it was hoped that an alliance could be brokered with them. Edward sent emissaries to make contact with the Mongol leader, Abaqa Khan. These entreaties were successful in getting the Mongols to agree to an assault on Muslim forces centered around Aleppo, Syria, to the northeast of Acre. This was meant to serve as a distraction to Baibars, leaving the road to Jerusalem unsecured.

So, in November of 1271, Edward led a force of English Crusaders augmented by contingents of Knights Templar and Knights Hospitaller to lay siege to the fortress of Qaqun. This citadel was of strategic importance because it was situated right between Acre and Jerusalem. If this fortress could be taken, it would serve as a launching pad for an assault on Jerusalem itself.

But things would not turn out as planned. Edward's motley crew was only able to reach the outskirts of the fortress. They could not even reach Qaqun itself since it was surrounded by fortified ditches of water. And with the fortress out of reach, the Crusaders were suddenly pushed back when reinforcements arrived.

Shortly after reaching Acre, Edward learned that the Mongols had backed away from their planned offensive in Aleppo, allowing the sultan's forces to retake the city by December 1271. Adding salt to Edward's wound, the sultan heard of all that had happened. He is said to have declared, "If so many men cannot take a house [the fortress of Qaqun], it seems unlikely that they will conquer the kingdom of Jerusalem." Nevertheless, Edward persevered. He persisted even when Hugh III, King of Jerusalem (he actually reigned from Cyprus), entered into a truce with Baibars.

Edward was brought up to view the struggle for the Holy Land as a zero-sum game, so he was frustrated to encounter the pragmatic realities on the ground. Acre was in no position to go to war with the sultan. Furthermore, merchants in the city had a lucrative trading relationship with the sultan's merchants. For Edward, such commercial ties with those he viewed as the "enemy" were appalling.

Yet, these were the realities on the ground. And even though the sultan and what remained of the Crusader kingdom of the Levant were often at odds, there were times when they could see eye to eye enough to agree to a cessation of hostilities. But Edward did not travel thousands of miles and waste a huge amount of money just so Acre could enter into a truce with the sultan. With Jerusalem just seventy miles from Acre, Edward could not give up his pledge to retake the "Holy City" and go home.

As such, Edward was highly dismayed when a ten-year truce was hammered out between the Crusader kingdom and the sultan. Edward, for one, most certainly was not going to wait ten years to reclaim Jerusalem. Edward's continued saber-rattling became a great source of agitation for both sides. Baibars came to understand the unique nuisance this interloper was creating and decided to take action.

Although historians are not able to verify the veracity of the account, according to Islamic chroniclers of the day, it is said that the sultan sent one of his own lieutenants to contact Edward. The lieutenant then proceeded to pretend he was party to a group of dissidents interested in switching sides and turning on the sultan. This was supposedly just to get Edward to let his guard down. The ruse is said to have worked, and Edward allowed an entire delegation that had been secretly dispatched by the sultan to visit his personal residence at Acre that summer.

Edward apparently thought he had gained valuable informants—spies he could use to undermine the sultan. Edward's special guests continued to work this ruse until sometime in June. They threw away their carefully crafted façade and turned on Edward. These supposed "friends" were actually a squad of assassins sent to remove a thorn from the sultan's side. One of these assassins managed to get Edward alone and pulled out a knife.

However, Edward was more tenacious than this hit squad had realized. Even though he was stabbed in the arm, he managed to use the other arm to pick up his sword and kill his attacker. Even so, it was soon learned that the blade used to stab Edward had been poisoned. This meant that what would have otherwise been a non-life-threatening injury had the potential to become lethal if the flow of poison was not stopped.

Edward's wound turned black from infection, and he actually drew up a will in case he did not survive. Fortunately for the future heir of England, Acre had some of the best doctors of the age. One of them was able to cut away the infected flesh and stop the flow of poison. This was no doubt a painful procedure for Edward to undergo, but it did save his life.

Even though the assassination had failed, Sultan Baibars was pleased with the results. After Edward's near-death experience, he had a change of heart and decided to give up the Crusade and return to England. After spending several weeks recovering, he set sail for home that September. In the meantime, his wife had given birth to a baby girl named Joan. The birth was greatly welcomed. Edward's son John, who was just a toddler at the time, had unexpectedly perished the previous summer.

Edward and his wife, Eleanor of Castile, had been through a lot. And both Edward and his wife, as it were, would spend their last days in Acre in a state of prolonged recuperation before they began the cumbersome journey back home. Once they finally set sail from Acre, they did not arrive at their next major port of call— the Italian island of Sicily—until that November.

From Sicily, they leapfrogged to Italy proper. Edward was not in a hurry for the long journey that awaited him, so he spent some time in the company of Charles of Anjou. While sojourning with Charles, Edward learned the news that his father, King Henry III, had passed away. Edward, fresh from a Crusade and an assassination attempt, was now the king of England.

Chapter 5 – The New King Takes Charge

"Now tell me, what does that mean to be noble? Your title gives you claim to the throne of our country, but men don't follow titles, they follow courage. Now our people know you. Noble, and common, they respect you. And if you would just lead them to freedom, they'd follow you. And so would I."

-William Wallace

After hearing the news of his father's passing, Edward found himself in a sad state of reflection. He knew his kingdom was in steady hands, as it was being overseen by the royal council, so he was not in a rush to return home. England faced no immediate threats at this time, and his succession to the throne was secure.

As such, Edward took his time on his overland return trip through Europe. Furthermore, there was apparently no need for a coronation since the entire royal court had already sworn their allegiance to Edward immediately after King Henry III's demise. The matter had apparently already been settled, and now all Edward had to do was show up and take his rightful place as king of England.

His arrival was preceded by a newborn son, which he and his wife dubbed Alfonso. He had been born in November of 1273 while Eleanor and Edward were still abroad. Edward actually had him shipped ahead of them that June. Once the infant reached England, he was united with his elder brother Henry. Sadly, Henry, the eldest child of Edward, would ultimately perish in October 1274 from a prolonged illness, making little Alfonso the presumptive heir to the throne.

Edward arrived at his royal court on August 2nd, 1274, and was officially given his crown on August 19th. Although he had already been hailed as king, an official coronation ceremony was still in the works. Unlike other coronations, when the crowning of a monarch was rushed right after the previous one had passed, there was plenty of time to prepare this time around.

This preparation for a grand ceremony would set a tradition and precedent for the future kings and queens of England. There was great and understandable relief among the court to have their rightful king back in their midst. And from the outset, Edward expressed some measure of concern for the people he ruled over. In November of 1274, for example, he sent a group of specially appointed commissioners all over England with the task of surveying the locals to see how they felt about local officials.

The surveys inquired as to "whether lords, or their stewards, or bailiffs of any kind" had mistreated or abused those under their charge. In other words, Edward was making a concerted effort to root out corruption among his underlings. It seems Edward had learned a valuable lesson from all of the uprisings that had occurred during his father's reign. He realized how crucial it was to have the general support of the populace at large rather than just having an inner circle of corrupt cronies.

The findings of the inquiry were complete by early 1275, and the new king took measures to reform his kingdom. It is worth noting that even while Edward was working to reform his kingdom, the neighboring Kingdom of Scotland was just beginning its tragic descent into tumult and turmoil. In that year, Queen Margaret, the wife of Scotland's King Alexander II, passed away.

Margaret was actually King Edward's sister. The death of the queen of Scots was a sad occasion for both Edward and the Scottish royal family, but it was not anything that would have completely disrupted the kingdom. It was the start of the tragedy, though, for just a few years later, in 1281, King Alexander's son, David, passed away. However, even worse was to come. David's elder brother—the heir to the Scottish throne, Alexander—died in 1284. Incredibly enough, the previous year of 1283 saw the death of King Alexander III's daughter.

Yes, in just a matter of a few short years, the king of Scotland had lost his wife and all of his children. With nowhere else to turn, the grieving king named a relation in Norway, a princess by the name of Margaret, as his heir. However, Margaret was just a child and was not yet ready to rule on her own. Nevertheless, Alexander III was in good health and figured he still had several years left to prepare.

But Alexander III's incredible spate of bad luck was not yet over. Shortly after he named Margaret as his heir, Alexander III himself perished in 1286. By then, the entire realm of Scotland, with only the vague promise of a small child in Norway as a prospective ruler, was thrown into considerable chaos. But we are getting a bit ahead of ourselves in the chronological order of events.

As it pertains to King Edward of England in the late 1270s, he was trying his best to reform his kingdom and not repeat the mistakes of his father. For the most part, he did. Rather than aggravating and alienating the masses, he presented himself as a monarch who was genuinely concerned about the people's welfare.

But by late 1275, he was more and more inclined to repeat one of his father's past perceived faults, as he was considering the issuance of a tax on his people. Edward's finances were in dismal shape ever since he returned from the Crusade, and he was looking for a means to replenish his depleted coffers. There was another solution besides taxing the populace. Llywelyn ap Gruffudd of Wales had since defaulted on his debts to the crown. But getting the crafty prince of Wales to pay up was another matter entirely.

In truth, Llywelyn was broke, but he would not admit this. Instead, he began bringing up past grievances. In the spring of 1274, he fired off a missive that stated, "The money is ready to be paid to your attorneys, provided that you compel the earl of Gloucester, Humphrey de Bohun and the other Marchers to restore to us the lands they have unjustly occupied."

Llywelyn was referring to certain men of note who had seized land in Wales. Since Llywelyn was flat broke at the time, he wished to use these trespasses as an excuse for not paying. For Edward, this was absolutely unacceptable. Even though he wanted to appear as a kind and just monarch to his subjects, he felt he had to have a strong hand when dealing with an upstart like Llywelyn.

More complications in Edward and Llywelyn's relationship emerged when Llywelyn and his brother Dafydd ran afoul of each other. This was more than a mere brotherly dispute since the childless Llywelyn had designated his brother as his heir. In the aftermath of their falling out, Dafydd ended up seeking refuge in England, with his brother viewing him as nothing more than a fugitive.

Llywelyn rekindled bitter feelings in England when he suddenly decided to marry the daughter of the deceased troublemaker Simon de Montfort. Montfort's daughter was yet another woman named Eleanor, not to be confused with either Edward's mother or his own wife of the same name. Llywelyn apparently planned to produce a new heir with Eleanor de Montfort and cut Dafydd out of the picture entirely.

The very name of Montfort no doubt brought chills to Edward's spine, as he was forced to recall his captivity at Montfort's hands. So, with the renegade brother Dafydd cozying up with Edward's court and Llywelyn cozying up with the hated Montfort's daughter, Wales and England had once again become at odds with each other.

Edward would intervene in the most direct way imaginable. He had Eleanor de Montfort's ship intercepted as it attempted to cross the English Channel from France to Wales. Eleanor de Montfort was then subsequently taken prisoner and held captive on King Edward's orders. Llywelyn and his new bride barely had time to exchange their vows (in fact, it is said they were wed by proxy) before she was ferreted off by Edward and held hostage. If relations were already bad enough, this act certainly would not have made them any better.

But despite the increasing hostility, Edward extended one more olive branch to Llywelyn. Right at the onset of the new year of 1276, he issued a call for Llywelyn to meet him in Westminster no later than April so that Llywelyn could officially pay homage. Llywelyn had not yet paid homage to the king; he was the only notable figure in Britain to have not done so.

Edward no doubt considered this occasion to be an opportunity for Llywelyn to officially submit. But despite the tradition of paying homage to a new monarch, Llywelyn was a no-show. April came and went, and Llywelyn was nowhere to be seen. Relations continued to deteriorate. On November 12th, 1276, Llywelyn was declared "a rebel and disturber of the peace," and war against him was affirmed. Edward had already been aiding the rebel Dafydd ap Gruffudd in his struggle against his brother in a kind of proxy war, but Edward was now ready to openly send in his own troops.

The main invasion force arrived in July 1277, with Edward sending some 15,500 soldiers to storm into Wales. For all of the lead-up to this climatic exchange, the battle that followed was nearly nonexistent. The armed forces that Llywelyn could muster were only a small fraction of what Edward had, and he could not risk sending them into open combat, as they would be immediately annihilated. Making matters even more difficult for Llywelyn was the fact that Edward had ferried a substantial number of troops to the island of Anglesey, just to the northwest of Gwynedd.

Edward had essentially created the perfect launching base for a sustained assault on Gwynedd. Llywelyn was pragmatic enough to realize that he didn't stand a chance against this onslaught. As such, he agreed to negotiate with Edward. This led to the Treaty of Aberconwy, which was put into effect in November 1277. This reduced the defeated Llywelyn to only having control of the region of Gwynedd, a section of northwestern Wales. Even though he was relegated to just this small rump state, for the sake of pride, he was given the consolation of being able to at least retain the moniker of prince of Wales. Edward also returned Eleanor de

Montfort to Llywelyn. Shortly thereafter, Edward helped arrange the official wedding ceremony of the couple, which took place in an English cathedral in Worcester.

Dafydd, who was Edward's nominal ally during this struggle, ended up becoming very resentful of the final arrangements and inevitably felt shortchanged. Dafydd had wanted Gwynedd for himself, but according to the treaty, his brother's diminished kingdom would retain it. Much of the rest of Wales was usurped by the English. Dafydd couldn't help but feel betrayed and perhaps guilty since his own actions had resulted in the carving up and diminishing of Welsh control of Wales.

At any rate, this animosity over the Treaty of Aberconwy would lead to Edward once again launching a campaign in Wales in 1282. Llywelyn, apparently forgetting his differences with his brother, as well as the terms of the treaty, joined the revolt, along with several other Welsh warlords. Soon, open warfare ensued. It must be noted that Llywelyn was in a very sad and desperate place at the time. That year, his wife Eleanor died in childbirth, ending the one link he had to Edward.

Llywelyn was now around sixty years of age, so he likely felt he no longer had anything to lose and simply decided to roll the dice one final time. This time around, Edward was playing for keeps, and what was a limited operation on the part of the English turned into an all-out war. Llywelyn's forces were basically surrounded by December of 1282, and Llywelyn ap Gruffudd was killed during the struggle.

The principal instigator of this new revolt, Dafydd, took his brother's place as the prince of Wales, but the kingdom he inherited was shattered, and he became little more than a fugitive.

The invasion of Gwynedd was implemented in March of 1283. Unable to stand against the English army, Dafydd took off and retreated to the mountains to hide. Eventually, he wound up at the mountain stronghold of Castell y Bere. The English were able to track him down, and in late April, a tremendous siege of the fortifications ensued. Dafydd managed to elude his pursuers yet again; at the very last minute, he fled into the wilderness. But nevertheless, the king's men were determined to find him, even though it took them until June to track him down. This time around, there would be no escape for Dafydd. On June 28th, King Edward was able to announce that the so-called "Prince of Wales" and the "last of a treacherous line" had been captured at last.

After being held in captivity for a brief time, Dafydd was escorted to the town of Shrewsbury by late September. Here, he was tried and found guilty of not only treason but also of personally plotting Edward's death. These charges seem to be a bit of a stretch. Dafydd did indeed lead a revolt, but to say that he was personally plotting Edward's death is stretching the truth.

Nevertheless, Dafydd was sentenced to death, meeting his fate on October 2nd, 1283. He was tied to the tail of a horse and dragged through the town square of Shrewsbury. After this humiliating and painful exercise, Dafydd then had a noose put around his neck and hung from a scaffold. Fortunately for Dafydd, it seems that he breathed his last shortly thereafter. He would not have to experience the pain of his postmortem torture.

Even after he died by hanging, his punishment was not yet over. He was disemboweled, and his entrails were burned to ashes. After this, Dafydd was then quartered, with his arms and legs cut off. The severed limbs were sent to the "four corners of Edward's kingdom" so that Dafydd's quartered remains would serve as a reminder that Edward's kingdom and authority lived.

After Dafydd's quartering, his tormentors then chopped off his head. With Edward's enemy defeated, the king held a feast. And as was the custom of great conquerors who had just overcome their enemies, King Edward gave thanks for his victory over Llywelyn, Dafydd, and all those who had dared stand against him in Wales. This joyous occasion was followed by yet another joyous occasion—the birth of a new English prince.

King Edward's wife, Queen Eleanor, gave birth to a healthy baby boy on April 25th, 1284. This child, who was named after his father, would indeed go on to be noteworthy since it was ultimately Edward II who succeeded Edward I. And King Edward and his queen would come to realize that Edward II was the heir to the throne not long after he was born. The following August, the previous heir apparent—Alfonso—abruptly perished.

But as mentioned, even while Edward's kingdom was being secured, Scotland was in the midst of a succession crisis. In 1284, Alexander III, King of Scotland, had appointed the Maid of Norway to be his heir, only to perish the following year. It was then up to the upper echelon—the lords and barons—of Scottish society to determine what might happen next. These notables convened in the spring of 1286 and established a provisional council referred to as the Guardians of the Kingdom of Scotland.

Since Margaret, the Maid of Norway, was not in any position to rule over Scotland just yet, these guardians would ultimately attempt to safeguard the realm until she came of age. It seemed as good a course as any at the time, but unfortunately for Scotland, its spate of bad luck was not yet over. The Maid of Norway herself abruptly passed in 1290 at just six years of age. This ultimately threw Scotland into a true succession crisis. And it was a crisis that the crafty and cunning King Edward I was more than willing to insert himself into.

Chapter 6 – Taming a Spirit of Defiance

"The King of France—not satisfied with the treacherous invasion of Gascony, has prepared a mighty fleet and army, for the purpose of invading England and wiping the English tongue from the face of the Earth."

-King Edward I

After the death of Margaret, the Maid of Norway, the presumptive heir to the Scottish throne, King Edward detected an opening to widen his own kingdom. He announced that he would henceforth be known as the Lord Paramount of Scotland. He also announced his intention of holding a feudal court by the fall of 1292 to further determine Scotland's fate. Edward was still convinced that he could have his wishes for Scotland fulfilled.

At this point in his reign, Edward was a man who had seen both triumph and tragedy. Even though he had conquered Wales, he faced the terrible misfortune of his wife, Queen Eleanor, abruptly passing on November 28th, 1290. During one of their sojourns to Gascony, she contracted malaria, and she perished upon her return.

But as much as Edward was saddened by his wife's death, the year 1290, in many ways, marks the year that he went for broke.

Without the calming presence of his wife at his side, he let his fiery zeal loose, wherever it might take him. And it was on the heels of his wife's passing that Edward learned of the death of the presumptive heir to the Scottish throne—Margaret, Maid of Norway.

This had deep implications for not only Scotland but also England since Edward's grand design included having his young son, Edward II, marry Margaret. This would then allow Edward II to one day rule over both England and Scotland. This plan was agreed upon by the temporary council—the Guardians of the Kingdom of Scotland—which was safeguarding the process of Scotland's dynastic succession.

All of these arrangements were underway when the Maid of Norway perished. After her passing, it was decided that a distant relative by the name of John Balliol could be a potential candidate. John had also been a member of the Guardians of Scotland. His involvement in the council added to his clout.

That's not to say there were no other claimants in this dynastic struggle. There were. The most vocal challenger against John Balliol's claims was a prominent Scotsman by the name of Robert Bruce, sometimes remembered as Robert the Bruce or Robert de Bruce. Despite Robert's standing with the Scottish, he was actually French in origin. His ancestor, also named Robert de Bruce, had taken part in William the Conqueror's army when he launched an invasion of England in 1066. Robert was convinced that his grandfather, a Scottish noble who was the 5th Lord of Annandale (also named Robert the Bruce), was a better pick for the role of king.

King Edward sought to forcibly coerce Scotland into the English fold. If fate would deny him his son's union, he would take matters into his own hands. He began to make demands and claims on Scotland as if it were already his vassal state and stated the Scottish king should be subservient to him.

The Scottish nobles had a ready-made excuse for ignoring Edward since there was currently no Scottish king on the throne. Edward wanted the Scottish king to pay him homage, but there was no Scottish king to do so. This situation changed in the fall of

1292 when the aforementioned John Balliol was proclaimed the new king of Scotland. As soon as his crown touched his brow, John Balliol had to deal with all of King Edward's incessant entreaties.

After all, John Balliol largely owed his crown to Edward's machinations. When John was chosen to be the new Scottish king, there was about equal support for the elder Robert the Bruce. However, Edward decisively put his thumb on the scale by picking Balliol as his choice. As such, Balliol immediately felt the need to repay Edward for his patronage.

One pressing demand was Edward's insistence that Scotland send both manpower and funds to aid England's battles. England had since become embroiled in hostilities with the French, and Edward insisted the Scottish render their aid. Scottish King Balliol also had the unenviable task of having to run to the English parliament whenever Edward called him. Like a true puppet, it was soon clear that Edward was pulling Balliol's strings.

As this appearance of English domination became ever evident, the Scottish people became more disheartened by Balliol's regime. They began calling him nothing more than a "Toom Tabard." It roughly means "Empty Coat" in English. The people saw John Balliol's nice and fancy royal coat, but due to England's dominance, they determined that it was just empty useless regalia. They believed their king was just a figurehead with no real authority of his own.

By the end of 1292, Robert the Bruce's fortunes had changed considerably. His grandfather, the 5th Lord of Annandale, chose to step down from his lordship, giving the title to Robert the Bruce's father, who happened to have the same name. This resulted in Robert the Bruce being given his dad's earldom of Carrick. It was a mere toehold in the world of nobility, but it was the first step in Robert the Bruce ultimately becoming a power to be reckoned with in his own right.

International events would put more strain and pressure on the tenuously fraught and fragile relationship between England and Scotland. The issue was with France, but it began over petty squabbles between regular English and French mariners, whose hostilities for each other had simply gotten out of control.

Although it is likely no one knows for sure how all of this played out, it is said that at some point in 1293, there was an isolated incident in which French and English sailors got into a physical altercation with each other. After the fighting was over, one of them had been killed. This isolated incident apparently ignited an all-out feud between English and French sailors. Even though on the governmental level, England and France were at peace, the individual sailors of these two nations were essentially waging war with each other.

Edward was greatly alarmed by these events and ended up convening a special delegation to investigate. Just prior to the start of the planned invasion, French ships launched an attack on England's Cinque Ports, attacking English sailors. The English apparently got the upper hand and managed to take several French sailors prisoner and seized much of their cargo. The king of France was on the verge of declaring war and fired off an angry missive to the English king, insisting that any prisoner of war, as well as cargo, needed to be returned immediately.

However, Edward was not willing to simply kowtow to the French monarch; instead, he pointed out the wrong done by both sides and suggested they make use of a neutral mediator by way of the pope. Yes, before the United Nations was ever even dreamed of, the pope often stood in as an international arbiter, playing a crucial role in moderating disputes within the Christian world. Since Edward sought a neutral, yet well-respected and powerful figure, he believed this to be the best course of action to take.

While Edward was waiting for France's response to his proposals, he continued on with his own personal affairs. That September, he married his oldest daughter, yet another Eleanor to Henry, Count of Bar. Henry was actually a count whose domain was in the eastern section of what today would be considered modern-day France. But back then, this chunk of French terrain was actually part of the western and central European conglomerate known as the Holy Roman Empire. If Edward's new son-in-law had been a French noble, perhaps these new marital relations would have been able to soften some of the rancor and discord, but as it was, it would do nothing to assuage the French king's animosity.

The real breakthrough—if there was to be one—rested on the shoulders of Edward's younger brother, Edmund. Edmund was deeply connected to the French nobility through his marriage to a French woman named Blanche of Artois. Blanche was the widowed mother of Jeanne of Navarre, who ended up wedding the French king, Philip IV. This essentially made Edward's brother Edmund none other than the stepfather of the queen of France.

Considering these extremely close ties, Edmund was dispatched to France to see if he could come to some sort of amicable agreement with the French king. During these confidential talks, they hatched a plot in which Edward would give up much of the territory of Gascony, as well as the aforementioned French prisoners of war that were being held. This would be done supposedly as a means of allowing the French king to "save face" and appear to be punishing the English. Edward supposedly had nothing to worry about because after this public spectacle was carried out, he would ultimately have the Gascon lands returned to him.

As preposterous as all of this might sound, Edward agreed to the scheme. Arrangements were made in early 1294 to put this plan into place. And to the shock of many of Edward's subjects, in February of 1294, evacuations of Gascony were underway, and English settlements were abandoned.

As a result, all of Gascony was in the French king's possession. Shortly thereafter, King Edward learned he had been double-crossed. France would not return Gascony. According to English chroniclers, once Edward realized his blunder, he literally "went red" as he fumed and raged over what had happened.

King Edward convened his parliament, and war against France was declared. Despite Edward's success in wars against weaker opponents such as Wales, taking on France would be no easy task. And he would need plenty of manpower and resources to do it. It was for this reason that Edward began forcing the Scottish to help the English fight in their war against France.

This situation would serve as a catalyst, making relations between England and Scotland go from bad to worse. And in addition to England's general harassment and abuse of Scottish citizens, John Balliol was pressured enough to switch sides. In July of 1295, Scottish nobles convened the Council of 12. Twelve members of Scotland's upper echelon superseded John Balliol's authority and made the decision to not only end Scotland's military support of England but also hook up with the French.

Scottish dignitaries were sent to France to forge ties. Referred to as the Auld Alliance, this was nothing short of a bid to forge a Franco-Scottish alliance to defeat the English. Since this was tantamount to an act of war, Edward's response was immediate. He confiscated all Scottish landholdings in England and then sent his army directly into Scotland that December.

Robert the Bruce stepped aside while this invasion of Scotland occurred, apparently not wanting any part of it. He remained holed up in Carlisle Castle as if he was nothing more than an innocent bystander. The more cynical among us might surmise that Bruce's strategy was to let his enemies—the English and other Scottish nobles—duke it out so that he could later rise up over the wreckage that ensued. At any rate, by January of 1296, Edward had amassed a large army to take on the Scottish revolt.

That March, after learning of Scottish assaults on Carham and even Robert the Bruce's castle, Edward ordered some eight thousand of his troops to surround the Scottish town of Berwick. Even though thousands of troops surrounded the city walls, the denizens of Berwick showed incredible defiance. Before engaging in hostilities, Edward gave them an opportunity to surrender, most likely assuming that they would. There was obviously no way this weakly defended city would stand up to a sizeable English army.

Nevertheless, showing either audacious bravery or reckless stupidity, the people of Berwick not only refused to surrender but also began shouting insults at the English. Upon seeing the monarch, it is said that some even turned around and dropped their pants before shaking their rear ends in his direction. Yes, they made use of the most universally understood gesture of disgust, contempt, and disregard for King Edward by "mooning" him.

Edward unleashed his soldiers on the city. They smashed right through the poorly defended city walls and flooded into Berwick. As bold as these citizens were, they barely had a chance. The scene did not even remotely resemble a battle; it was nothing short of a bloodbath, with English troops wantonly killing Berwick's citizens. After having taken the city of Berwick and smashing its city walls, King Edward immediately began to rebuild and fortify the city's defenses, not for the sake of the Scottish who lived there but to turn it into his own fortress and forward base for further assaults into the Scottish interior.

When John Balliol became aware of the massacre of Berwick's citizenry, he officially disavowed any previous oath of loyalty to King Edward. If it wasn't clear before, it was clear now that John Balliol had finally broken the chains that bound him to the English king. However, John Balliol's freedom from Edward wouldn't last long. His fate would be determined that April when Scottish rebels slammed into English forces at Dunbar, about thirty miles from Berwick. Dunbar was of strategic importance because of the Castle of Dunbar, which was the home base of important Scottish nobles in the region.

Edward was busy making Dunbar his next target when Scottish troops attempted to intervene. Rather than save Dunbar, all the Scottish forces did was serve as a distraction. The Scottish rebels were unable to stand up to England's professional soldiers, and they were utterly decimated in open combat.

After seizing Dunbar, Edward had yet another strategic Scottish outpost under his control. He was also able to take three Scottish earls who had been holed up in the castle as captives. Edward was then able to easily take control of the nearby towns of Jedburgh and Roxburgh. After this, he made his way to Edinburgh, which gave in to his demands after just a few days of being besieged.

Stirling, another city, didn't even try to resist Edward's assault. He arrived to find the city defenders had engaged in a preemptive retreat. The warriors were gone, and the city was wide open for Edward to take. Soon enough, it became clear to John Balliol and the other rebels that their cause was lost.

As such, on July 8th, 1296, Balliol and those in his immediate circle formally surrendered from the Scottish city of Montrose, where they had holed up. John Balliol hoped that Edward would be lenient on him and perhaps even allow him to simply resign from his post as king and quietly retire. But as soon as John was forced to take off his crown, the deposed king was marched right off to the Tower of London.

By August, Edward was officially in control of Scotland. He had no intention of installing another "empty coat" puppet, making it clear that he would be the top authority over Scottish affairs. Robert the Bruce was rewarded for complying with the English, regaining his territories in Carrick and Annandale. However, his aspiration to one day become king of Scotland was dashed.

It has been said that the matter was brought up directly to King Edward at one point, only to have the king callously respond, "Do you think we have nothing better to do than to win kingdoms for you?" No, Edward had no intention of invading Scotland by force of arms just to install another king on the Scottish throne. As far as he was concerned, he was now the king of Scotland and England.

Edward further showed his contempt for the idea of the Scottish monarchy by seizing Scottish royal regalia, such as the Seal of Scotland, which he handed off to the colonial governor he installed in the region. King Edward handed the Scottish royal seal to the new governor as a lark, stating, "A man does good business when he rids himself of a turd."

Nevertheless, even though Scotland, which Edward had so flippantly referred to as being nothing more than a "turd," had been beaten, the Scottish people's spirit of defiance had not been defeated.

Chapter 7 – All of the King's Horses and All of the King's Men

"We fight not for glory, nor for wealth, nor honour but only and alone for freedom which no good man surrenders but with his life."

-Robert the Bruce

In the aftermath of Scotland's subjugation to English authority, there were still smoldering flames of resistance just waiting to properly ignite. England was still at war with France and had received a troubling blow on January 30th, 1297 when it was learned that nearly an entire English army had been decimated during an attempt to retake control of Gascony. In the midst of all this, a new Scottish freedom fighter emerged in the form of one William Wallace.

Wallace was a man of mediocre nobility who rose to fame through his own personal struggle against the English occupation of Scotland. Scotland was being run by Edward's appointed cronies, such as his colonial governor, as well as several sheriffs who controlled various regions. These men had no love for Scotland, and the Scottish people soon began to groan under the weight of their oppression. It was a feeling of utter desperation, something that William Wallace had come to know all too well.

Sometime in the month of May, Wallace attended Mass, only to walk out of the church service to step right into a whole lot of trouble. It was not trouble of his own making but a byproduct of the brutal English occupation of his homeland. He and some friends left the church, only to be ridiculed by a group of English troops. Wallace was made a target of ridicule because of the finely crafted knife he wore on his belt—something that English authorities did not think Scots should openly possess.

As Wallace stood outside the church doors, one of the Englishmen, seeing the knife, shouted at Wallace, "What should a Scot do with so fair a knife—as the priest said who last f****ed your wife!" Wallace had just married a local woman by the name of Marion Braidfute, and to hear coarse words thrown in her direction—even from a stranger—made Wallace's blood boil. Nevertheless, he tried to ignore the taunts, but the English soldiers continued their jeers and threatened Wallace and his companions.

Although Wallace was completely outnumbered, he made the fateful decision to fight back. With lightning speed, Wallace had his weapon in hand and used it to slice the sword arm of his lead antagonist. Wallace and his few friends had to fight in close quarters, as they were confined to the narrow thoroughfare in front of the church, which meant the English could not take full advantage of their numerical superiority.

Wallace and his comrades managed to carefully fight their way out of the mob. As the English troops slipped and fell in pools of their own blood, Wallace and company were able to make a break for it and took off running. They immediately headed to Wallace's home. His wife let them in and locked the door. After a very brief explanation of what was happening, Wallace and his allies exited out the back of the house and took off to hide in the surrounding wilderness.

If accounts of this incident can be believed, dozens of English troops were killed by Wallace and his friends as they made their escape. If that was the case, one can only imagine the sense of reprisal that was in the air immediately afterward. And unfortunately, without Wallace around to exact their wrath on, the authorities chose to target his wife instead.

In this closely knit Scottish community, they were able to find out everything about Marion Braidfute, and English enforcers were soon at her door. It has been said that Marion was "put to death on the spot" for allowing Wallace to escape. The death of his wife would turn Wallace from a fugitive into a fierce and determined freedom fighter, one who would not rest until the English occupation of Scotland was overthrown.

William Wallace's first act of vengeance was to launch a daring raid on the residence of the sheriff responsible for his wife's death. Wallace is said to have killed the sheriff, stabbing him to death as he slept. Wallace and his cohorts were then able to retreat back into the nearby wooded region of Selkirk Forest, where they made their secret hideout. From here, he would galvanize more Scottish rebels to join his struggle, and by August, he had a veritable army of freedom fighters at his disposal, with which he marched to Scone, Scotland.

Here, Wallace and his followers would take a direct stand against the English army that had been dispatched to crush them. To get to Wallace's troops situated in northern Scotland, the English had to cross the River Forth, which separated northern and southern Scotland. This meant crossing over Stirling Bridge, which spanned across the river. But as the English began their crossing in early September, they would have none other than Wallace and his band of freedom fighters to greet them on the other side.

Wallace was outnumbered, not for the first time in his life. He and his men were just a fraction of the size of the English. Yet, once again, Wallace was able to make use of ingenious strategy when sheer numbers failed him. Since the English were forced to cross the bridge, they could not make use of the main bulk of their army. The bridge is said to have been so narrow that only two men could cross side by side at a time.

Wallace fully anticipated this and had a plan to make full use of it. He waited until only a small portion of the English had crossed the bridge before he signaled his warriors to attack. The English were caught by surprise and forced into a chaotic retreat back to the bridge. Wallace then continued the assault, hacking and slashing the English to death as they were forced to fight, confined on the narrow bridge. After what was left of the English army managed to cross back to the other side, the bridge was destroyed.

So, it was on September 11th, 1297, during the Battle of Stirling Bridge, that William Wallace managed to nearly annihilate an entire English army. It was a stunning and decisive victory for Wallace and all of his Scottish compatriots. And it was a terrible blow to King Edward. Things looked grim. War raged in France, and now he had a formidable guerrilla army roving about unchecked in northern Scotland.

King Edward would receive some good news the following month when he was able to enter into a temporary ceasefire of sorts with France. The two parties entered into an official two-month truce on October 9th, 1297. This gave Edward just enough time and breathing room to focus all of his attention on the Scottish revolt. At this point, Wallace's rebellion had spread throughout Scotland. Roxburgh and even mighty Berwick had been subdued.

By the end of the month, Wallace and his growing army of followers made their way across the Scottish border and into England itself. Soon, English residents of the counties of Northumbria and Cumbria were being subjected to vicious raids conducted by the Scotts. It seemed clear that Edward would need more than a couple of months to take on this massive insurgency. And as fate would have it, he would get more than two months.

In January of 1298, just as Edward was scrambling his troops into position to face the encroaching Scots, Edward and the king of France agreed to enter into a two-year truce. According to the terms of the truce, both sides would submit to the pope as a neutral arbiter over the ultimate fate of Gascony upon the agreement's expiration. This was, in fact, what Edward's intention had been all along. Elated with the news that he could end his expenditure of troops and resources in France, King Edward immediately redirected all of his attention to William Wallace and his growing rebellion.

As the English forces marched north, Wallace and his army slipped back over the border and proceeded to disappear into the wilderness. It was not until July 21st, 1298, that Edward received word that Wallace and his whole army were located some twenty miles west of his position. Edward drove his forces west and managed to catch sight of Wallace's ragtag army the next day. The English army again had the numerical advantage, but Wallace and his fellow Scottish freedom fighters literally had the high ground since they were positioned on hilly terrain.

Wallace no doubt hoped the English could be tricked into a risky charge, which would allow him and his forces to make the most of their situation. However, King Edward, who at this point was in his fifties, had been in more than enough battles to realize the risk of such tactics. He approached the situation with caution and had his men set up camp in the vicinity of nearby Falkirk.

Edward was initially hesitant to advance but was ultimately overruled by his generals, who insisted they must dispatch the enemy as quickly and decisively as possible. This kicked off what would later be known as the Battle of Falkirk. As the English charged the Scottish positions, Wallace determined to hold the high ground and had his infantry arranged in tight square formations. Initially, the Scottish warriors were quite good at pushing the English back. However, the English army had a surprise for Wallace and company in the form of their longbowmen.

The longbow was a fairly new innovation at this time, and William Wallace and his compatriots were entirely unprepared for its devastatingly long reach. Suddenly, arrows were being shot from a great distance in all directions, and Wallace's previously tight formations were being rapidly chipped away.

As Wallace's infantry began to disintegrate, the English army again charged the Scottish positions. This time, they broke through the Scottish lines. Wallace's army was ultimately crushed, but he and a small fraction of his followers managed to escape, causing the war against the Scottish rebels to devolve into more or less a manhunt for the principal agitator—William Wallace. Edward was victorious, but without William Wallace to show for it, his victory would remain inconclusive.

Nevertheless, after leaving behind several garrisons of troops at strategic locations in Scotland, Edward returned to England that October. He probably returned too soon because shortly after, Scottish rebels managed to seize the fortified compound of Stirling Castle. The Scottish militants were neither willing nor able to wage full-scale battles after their defeat at Falkirk and largely employed hit-and-run tactics, launching daring ambushes and raids from their strongholds.

In the spring of 1299, with the continued turmoil and uncertainty in Scotland as a backdrop, King Edward convened parliament at Westminster. The discussion wasn't just on Scotland. They also spoke about the pope, who had recently determined that France should return the lands in Gascony that it had previously seized back to England. But even though the pope had come up with this supposed solution, the French had not yet agreed to it.

Edward figured this would set the stage for a positive convening of parliament. However, his feathers were sorely ruffled when the conversation turned toward his commitment to reform, specifically the need to uphold two important texts—the Magna Carta and the Charter of the Forest.

The famed Magna Carta limited the powers of the previously absolute English monarch, and it had been passed several decades prior to Edward's arrival on the throne.

The Charter of the Forest was a kind of "complementary" text to the Magna Carta, which guaranteed the average subject would have access to the royal forests. It might sound a bit odd to the uninitiated, but this was a big deal to the English at the time since a huge chunk of England was designated as royal forests owned by the king. Therefore, it was imperative that the citizenry have access to the king's forests in order to hunt food, gather lumber, use water, and utilize whatever other resources might be available.

By the late 1290s, the subject matter of these documents had taken precedence once again, and the king was being pressured to reconfirm his commitment to them both. During this particular session of parliament, due to the lengthy discussion of these matters, Edward became so frustrated that he suddenly declared he would be leaving and would return to speak further the next day. The next day, however, he was a no-show. It seems a medieval monarch such as Edward might not have had the absolute power to arbitrarily punish members of parliament for merely speaking out, but he did retain the power to simply not show up at all.

The reformers were frustrated, and protests soon took place in London. The unrest was troublesome enough for Edward that he finally gnashed his teeth at his subjects. On April 2nd, 1299, he issued a decree that local officials should "arrest, try and punish persons congregating by day and night, and speaking ill of the king."

Edward most certainly recalled all of the messy revolts his father had to put down and realized that he really could not ignore the situation any longer. As such, he convened a new parliament so that the reform issues could be discussed. Yet, even after a full convening of parliament, the reformers were still not quite satisfied.

Shortly afterward, Edward received some good news. He learned the king of France had decided to recognize his right to control Gascony. In order to seal the deal and confirm the newfound friendship between the two kings, a dynastic marriage was proposed between Edward II and Philip IV's daughter, Isabella. Isabella was just a small child at the time, so this particular engagement would be a long one, as she could not marry until she came of age. King Edward, who was a widower, would wed King Philip's sister, Margaret. Margaret was seventeen at the time, so she was deemed old enough for her marriage to the sixty-year-old English monarch shortly after her arrival in England that September.

Their wedding was a cause for great celebration and served as a great distraction from both the brewing conflict in Scotland and other domestic problems. Nevertheless, as it pertained to Scotland, Edward had not forgotten the revolt he had only partially put down. He soon made plans to launch another all-out invasion of Scotland that November.

In the meantime, Scotland was in a turmoil of its own making. The resistance was still alive, but it was faltering. Wallace, who had previously been recognized as a "guardian of Scotland," was forced to step down in the aftermath of Falkirk and was reduced to a mere guerilla warlord. He could still launch some fairly stunning hit-and-run attacks but was no longer able to field an army large enough to take on the English in open combat. The true leadership of Scotland was shared by two Scottish notables: Robert the Bruce and a man named John Comyn.

Robert the Bruce had since fallen out with English authorities and was very much considered a part of the rebellion. John Comyn was a Scottish noble whose family had supported the deposed former Scottish king, John Balliol. The leadership of Scotland was divided between these two men. Things looked very grim for Scotland in regard to its war of independence, and when it was learned that King Edward had made peace with France, the situation looked a whole lot worse.

Scotland had sought to align itself with France in the hopes their alliance would put enough pressure on England to reconsider an all-out invasion of Scotland. It was also hoped that if peace was brokered between France and England, perhaps generous terms could be created for Scotland as well. But Edward did not want to make concessions to Scotland a part of the bargain.

Under pressure from France and the pope, Edward finally agreed to release the deposed king, John Balliol, from the Tower of London. He was allowed to peacefully cross the English Channel and was put into the custody of papal authorities who met him in France. John Balliol would continue to live out his days in exile. Nevertheless, some of Balliol's supporters held out hope that their exiled king might return. The more pragmatic and realistic Scottish realized this would not be the case and instead backed either John Comyn or Robert the Bruce.

Relations between these two leading lights of Scotland had become fraught with tension. At one point, they were so incensed they even came to literal blows against each other, with John

Comyn seizing Robert the Bruce by the throat.

At any rate, both men knew that a terrible storm was headed their way now that Edward was at peace with the French king and his troops were no longer bogged down in France. Scotland would feel the full brunt of an English invasion. And the Scottish certainly bore witness to a time of absolute terror and strife, as all the king's horses and all the king's men sought to bring Scotland to heel once again.

Chapter 8 – Renewed Hostilities in Scotland

"Historians from England will say I am a liar, but history is written by those who have hanged heroes."

-Robert the Bruce

Edward's second full-fledged assault on Scotland began at the end of 1299. That December, Edward arrived at the English outpost of Berwick to oversee the buildup of arms. Berwick was an English stronghold in Scotland and would serve as a forward base for the larger invasion. King Edward rang in the New Year at Berwick and headed back to England in early January. Due to various other matters Edward had to deal with at home, he would ultimately wait until the following year to strike.

Edward led a major offensive back into Scotland in 1301. This expedition saw King Edward's son, Edward II, leading a portion of the troops, while King Edward personally led the rest. Prince Edward II's forces managed to seize Robert the Bruce's Turnberry Castle. Edward first heard of this feat on September 2nd and is said to have personally given his thanks to God in Glasgow Cathedral. Shortly thereafter, King Edward's forces possessed the strategic castle of Bothwell.

Edward I's forces were closing in from the east and Edward II's forces were closing in from the west—this father and son duo was essentially trying to destroy the Scottish rebels through a powerful pincer maneuver. But the pincer was never fully completed, and these efforts were disrupted on September 7th when Scottish forces suddenly made their presence known right outside of Lochmaben Castle. The English garrison stationed there was taken completely by surprise, and the assault forced Edward II's troops to cease their attempted encirclement of Scotland so they could head southward to relieve Lochmaben. This disruption prevented the two ends of the English forces from meeting, and the planned pincer would never come to fruition.

Rebel leader William Wallace was still at large and wreaking havoc through guerilla warfare and hit-and-run tactics. It seemed that no matter how many troops Edward put in place and no matter how many fortresses he seized, Wallace's shadowy rebel army was slowly bleeding him dry. Running low on both manpower and resources, Edward seemed to acknowledge how fruitless his campaign was in 1302, as he agreed to a brief truce with Wallace and the rebels.

Robert the Bruce, on the other hand, was another story. Robert the Bruce could not run and hide in the wilderness and launch a guerilla warfare campaign. Bruce had to stand and face Edward directly. As such, he was forced to promise his loyalty to England once again.

The exact timeline of when Bruce "surrendered" to English authority is not entirely clear, but it is believed that sometime in early 1302, Bruce showed up at the gates of the English-controlled Lochmaben Castle and willfully surrendered to the English stationed there. Edward received word of Bruce's surrender that January and was quite pleased to hear it. Maintaining his celebratory mood, Edward went on to host a Round Table tournament on January 20th, 1302.

In the following year, with his military forces refurbished, Edward ended his truce with the rebels and launched another offensive against the Scottish in 1303. This time around, Edward planned to succeed.

Just prior to the campaign, Edward had gone to great lengths to raise funds by any means possible. Old debts were demanded to be repaid, and certain tariffs were put in place on foreign merchants. With all of the money Edward amassed, he put together a huge army that once again consisted of two main battalions—one under the charge of his son, Edward II, and the other under the guidance of his own hand. It was determined that he and his son would attack Scotland simultaneously on two fronts. With these battlelines drawn, King Edward took the army he commanded and headed into Scotland's eastern territories, while his son penetrated Scotland from the west.

Robert the Bruce was once again made a loyal vassal of King Edward and forced to provide thousands of troops to join the fight. One can only imagine how conflicted Robert the Bruce must have been to recruit Scotsmen to fight fellow Scotsmen, but he no longer had much of a choice in the matter.

Another major aspect of King Edward's 1303 campaign in Scotland revolved around a planned taking of Scottish leader John Comyn's stronghold in northern Scotland. This, of course, involved crossing the dreaded River Forth, and the disaster of the Battle of Stirling Bridge was still very much on King Edward's mind. His initial plan was an ingenious one. Rather than struggling to cross the river via the traditional crossing, Edward was determined to make his own.

He tapped skilled engineers and asked them to make a pontoon bridge that could be strategically placed over the river wherever the king chose. King Edward would then be able to have his engineers place a pontoon downriver in a much more secure and stable environment, which would better facilitate the crossing of the English army.

The construction of the bridges (for more than one prototype was made) would take a few months and cost a lot of money for parts, labor, and transport of needed materials. Ironically enough, by the time the bridges were made, it was decided that the immediate situation around Stirling was secure enough to use the conventional crossing that was already in place. No pontoon bridge was required. King Edward and his men made that fateful crossing in the summer of 1303.

After reaching Stirling, Edward's forces advanced to Perth. They remained there for well over a month to await much-needed supplies. With their food, medicines, and armaments replenished, Edward's force continued the campaign. That July, the king's forces reached the port of Montrose. Once Montrose was secure, they were able to link up with the English navy, which dropped off artillery that was subsequently used to demolish the fortified town of Brechin that August.

King Edward and company then took Aberdeen on August 23rd but had to regroup since Edward's infantry had become severely depleted from casualties and desertions. Due to a lack of sufficient funds, many of the infantry sneaked away from battle. Edward fired off a letter to his exchequer in which he glumly stated, "If we cannot make these payments, they [the infantrymen] will go back to their own parts, as they are already doing from day to day."

Edward was voicing the growing concern that poorly paid troops would rather risk the trek through hostile enemy territory to reach their familiar "parts" of England than fight for inadequate pay. This was indeed an issue with which Edward had to contend. The matter was solved on August 28th when ships sailed into Aberdeen and dropped off cash. With his infantry secured, Edward took the bulk of his army and marched deep into Scotland.

By September, he had reached Moray Firth, and by the following week, he was besieging the very fortress of John Comyn, the last visible leader of the struggle for Scottish independence. John Comyn was still on the loose with a small army in central Scotland, but Edward was prepared to take his time if need be. By November, he had moved his army onto the northern bank of the Forth in the vicinity of Dunfermline Abbey. The king's son, Prince Edward II, amassed his forces at the Tay River near the town of Perth.

The Scottish rebels were now in the precarious position of basically hiding in the open, wedged between two hostile armies that had already overrun Scottish strongholds. John Comyn and his forces knew they had already lost. Since there was no real hope of them overcoming the English, the best they could do was seek to negotiate. And soon enough, negotiations between the two parties were underway.

The best possible outcome for John Comyn and his cohorts would have been complete amnesty. They were not able to secure such a thing, but they did get close to it. Edward was weary of war and granted John Comyn a pledge that "there would be no loss of life or limb, lands or liberty" if he and his troops immediately surrendered to the English. As it turns out, the severest penalty would be a temporary exile for those who were deemed to be the most egregious offenders.

As for John Comyn himself, as long as he publicly paid homage to Edward, he would be taken back into the English fold. This was achieved in February of 1304 when the once-proud John Comyn was made to literally bow before King Edward of England. With the previous Scottish guardians John Comyn and Robert the Bruce both under England's sway, all that remained were a few Scottish warlords. Edward went after the first of these holdouts, Stirling Castle, in 1304.

Stirling was indeed a formidable fortress, but Edward was now free to focus all of his might on this one objective. He had the best in siege artillery, which had been shipped to him from all corners of his dominion, and he was fully prepared to completely level Stirling Castle to the ground if need be. In one of the earliest uses of gunpowder weaponry, the formidable fortress was reduced to rubble over several weeks. The sight of these new weapons taking potshots at the fortress became almost a source of amusement for Edward as he watched the action from afar.

Incredibly, the denizens of Stirling endured twelve full weeks of this onslaught before they finally decided to surrender. Even so, Edward insisted that the surrender would have to wait until he could test out more of his new weapons. Edward has long been criticized for this seemingly callous response, but at the time, Edward and most of his peers seemed to feel he was justified due to everything the Scots had put him through.

On July 24th, the formal surrender of Stirling Castle was approved. It was a theatrical affair, in which the defenders came out of the castle groveling at the feet of their conquerors, barefoot and with ashes (the classic sign of humility) smeared across their foreheads. Edward respected ritual routines and was apparently moved enough to let his wrath subside. Fortunately for the denizens of Stirling, Edward declared he would be merciful.

Edward could not have been happier, and he even marked the occasion by hosting yet another bout of royal tournament games in celebration of the outcome. However, there was only one main Scottish antagonist left for King Edward to deal with—the rebel leader William Wallace.

Chapter 9 – King Edward and the Fate of William Wallace

"We come here with no peaceful intent, but ready for battle, determined to avenge our wrongs and set our country free."

-William Wallace

With the capitulation of the main rebel forces in the summer of 1304, Scottish freedom fighter William Wallace had become little more than a fugitive with a small armed band holed up in the most remote parts of Scotland. It took about a year of searching, but in the following summer of 1305, William Wallace was finally tracked down and taken into custody. Despite all of Edward's gains in the region, it was not an easy task. Wallace knew all of the back roads and backwoods of his homeland well enough to elude his captors almost indefinitely.

For this reason, Edward finally broke down and resorted to subterfuge and deception in order to finally lay his hands on Wallace. Edward recruited a Scottish knight whose name comes down to us as Sir John de Menteith to do his dirty work for him. In this truly elaborate bit of intrigue, Menteith actually recruited his nephew to hook up with Wallace's guerrilla band. Upon joining the group, his nephew reported back to his uncle about all of Wallace's movements.

With this intelligence, John and a group of other men were able to zero in on where Wallace was staying. They snuck right into his house late at night to find him fast asleep in the arms of a female companion. These intruders wanted to take Wallace alive, but it would prove quite challenging to do so, for once Wallace was awakened to this intrusion, he was ready to fight to the death. Even though he did not have a weapon, he grabbed a hold of the interlopers and began to tear them apart with his bare hands.

First, Wallace seized the neck of the first person who approached him and throttled him with his iron grip, breaking the man's spine in the process. He then turned to his next opponent and pummeled him so hard his skull cracked open, releasing a fountain of bloody gore as the man dropped to the ground dead. The rest of the men were able to finally lay hands on Wallace, although it was not easy. They had Wallace for the moment, but as hard as he was struggling, it seemed they would not be able to hold him for long.

Wallace probably would have fought to the bitter end had it not been for the deception of John de Mentieth. At this point, Menteith stepped forward and lied through his teeth, shouting that the English army had the place surrounded. He then further lied by promising Wallace safe passage upon his surrender and that he would be taken under Menteith's own protection at Dunbarton Castle. Wallace trusted Mentieth, so after Menteith gave his word, he finally relented and allowed himself to be bound hand and foot.

However, once Wallace was escorted outside and saw that there was no large contingent of English troops standing around the property, he realized that he had been deceived. And this sense of betrayal was only further confirmed when Menteith and his entourage continued riding south, well past the promised refuge of Dunbarton Castle.

The men knew how dangerous their captive was, and it is said they only traveled under cover of night lest they attract the attention of Wallace's remaining guerilla fighters. If Wallace's compatriots had been alerted to what was happening, it would not have taken much for them to swoop down and free their leader.

At any rate, Wallace eventually reached London and was promptly turned over to the English authorities.

Upon his arrival in London, a terrible fate awaited William Wallace. Even though King Edward was quite merciful to the likes of John Comyn and Robert the Bruce, he was prepared to unleash his full vengeance upon William Wallace. Part of the reasoning behind this was nothing more than Wallace being a convenient target of which to make an example. Wallace was a man of lower rank who had risen to prominence through the notoriety of his rebellion. He wasn't as useful as a rehabilitated John Comyn or Robert the Bruce was.

The reasoning behind dropping the hammer so hard on Wallace was also largely a matter of pure and simple revenge. After all, it was Wallace who had humiliated the English army at the Battle of Stirling Bridge, and Edward, ever mindful of appearances, wanted to show the world that he had bested William Wallace—the beast of Stirling Bridge—once and for all. As such, given all of these mitigating circumstances, William Wallace was certainly in for a rough ride when he arrived arrival in London on August 22nd, 1305.

King Edward had arranged for Wallace to participate in a kind of show trial, in which he would be roundly condemned with practically no opportunity to mount any kind of defense. This was done to satisfy Edward's twisted sense of pride and to create an elaborate demonstration of farcical justice for both the French king and the pope, who had previously attempted to arbitrate peace between Scotland and England.

On August 23rd, 1305, William Wallace was taken to Westminster to stand trial. Wallace was made to sit on a bench in the back of the courtroom while the charges against him were leveled. Adding to the absurdity, it is said that a crown of laurel leaves was placed on Wallace's head, apparently in mockery of his pretenses to be a great leader.

It is strangely ironic to note that King Edward would subject Wallace in a manner somewhat reminiscent of how the Romans treated Christ since the king was a zealous Christian. While envisioning the crown of leaves on Wallace's head, one cannot help but think of Christ bearing the crown of thorns. But, of course, there are many differences as well. Jesus preached a message of peace, love, and non-violence, while Wallace was a Scottish warlord fighting a bloody revolution.

Once Wallace's trial commenced, a series of charges was leveled against him. First, he was accused of killing the sheriff of his hometown of Lanark, Scotland. This was true, but it was conveniently forgotten that the sheriff had killed Wallace's wife. Wallace was then accused of rampaging through Scotland, raiding towns, and killing innocents in horrible bloodbaths. It was indeed a bloody war, but again, only Wallace's supposed abuses merited any mention. What was viewed as the worse crime of all was saved for last. It was stated that Wallace had sought to commit the high crime of treason by involving France in the conflict. William Wallace, like other Scottish notables, had indeed made entreaties to the French, yet for some reason, only Wallace was being made to pay the price for this perceived overreach.

Predictably enough, William Wallace was condemned to death at the end of the proceedings. He was to be hung and drawn and quartered. Similar to the Welsh warlord Dafydd ap Gruffudd before him, Wallace was to have his head and limbs removed and placed in various parts of the kingdom as a reminder to anyone else tempted to rebel.

This grisly sentence was carried out just about as soon as it was issued. Wallace was ushered out of the courtroom, had his clothes removed, and was then tied behind a horse, which dragged him through the streets. As he was dragged to the gallows where he would be hung, citizens gathered around to hurl verbal insults, rocks, and other debris at the passing form of William Wallace.

Upon reaching his destination, William Wallace was dragged onto the gallows and hung. However, he was not hung to death because just short of his expiration, the rope was cut. Wallace fell to the ground, gasping for air. He was about to pass out, so to prevent him from going unconscious, his tormentors poured cold water on him. His captors then sliced off his penis, causing the revived Wallace to howl in unimaginable pain. After this atrocity, Wallace's stomach was cut open, and his intestines were removed before being tossed into a bonfire.

It is said that Wallace only died when his heart was ripped out, still beating, from his chest. His body was then dismembered. His head was chopped off, and his limbs were removed with chunks of the torso still attached. In other words, he was "quartered" into four distinct pieces of bloody, gory flesh. The head and the four quartered pieces of William Wallace would be sent to various parts of Edward's domain and put on grisly display to serve as a warning to anyone who might consider crossing the king of England.

All of this, of course, is shocking beyond belief to modern sensibilities, and the sheer brutality serves to remind us of why people use the phrase, "I'm about to go medieval on you!" During the medieval age, —meting out justice (or vengeance) on your perceived opponent was indeed an altogether horrific affair.

Chapter 10 – Consolidating His Gains

"Praise God, who up to now has delivered me from all difficulties."

-King Edward I

With Scotland brought to heel, his nemesis William Wallace dead, peace secured with France, and Gascony restored, King Edward I had made unprecedented gains. However, despite his triumph, Edward realized he would have to engage in some sort of reconciliation with the Scottish people if there was going to be any real hope of lasting peace. As such, in September of 1305—right on the heels of the death of William Wallace—Edward convened a meeting of important Scottish notables in London.

After pouring all of his wrath out on William Wallace, King Edward and his government were quite polite and accommodating to their Scottish guests. Although to be safe, everyone present was absolutely mum on the prospect of Scottish kingship. Edward had made it clear that he would be the ultimate authority in Scotland. Nevertheless, most of the sheriffs Edward appointed to oversee various Scottish regions were local Scottish figures.

Edward had seemingly learned his lesson in regard to posting only English cronies in Scotland. He realized the locals would most likely listen to one of their own countrymen rather than a visiting English blowhard. And if this was enough to prevent another bloody and costly revolt, Edward had no problem with it. Edward now seemed right on track to consolidate his gains and keep the peace. The sixty-six-year-old king seemed to have finally gotten his kingdom in order.

But it was around this time that Robert the Bruce, who had previously been a useful tool of King Edward's, had rendered his service. On February 10th, 1306, Bruce ended up killing his former rival and former fellow guardian of Scotland, John Comyn. By most accounts, this was not a planned or premeditated murder but merely a tragic decision made in the heat of the moment.

On that fateful day in February, John and Robert agreed to meet each other, not to do battle but to attempt to mend fences and solve previous disagreements. Things did not go well, and the two began bickering over past perceived slights. When Comyn declared that Robert the Bruce was a "traitor" to Scotland, Bruce seemed to have lost his cool.

Bruce angrily got up and began to step away, but something in his mind suddenly snapped. Instead of getting away from the source of his frustration, he whirled around and sent his sword sailing right into John Comyn. It's unclear if Comyn was fatally injured at this point, but a comrade of Robert's immediately began hacking at Comyn as well, making sure to finish him off. Bruce then had the audacity to steal the slain Comyn's horse and use it to bolt off like a fugitive.

There have been some who have speculated that perhaps there was a little more to this story than was generally let on. It is possible Bruce hatched a plot with Comyn to lead a rebellion, and Comyn refused. If this did occur, Robert the Bruce may have chosen to silence Comyn out of fear that he would alert King Edward to his plans.

At any rate, Robert the Bruce's behavior did not look good, no matter how one might have tried to spin it. He obviously lost control and did something he should not have, and there was no way that King Edward could use a man who had committed such an act. Bruce seemed to have known that his fate was sealed, and he seemed to accept that the die had been cast. He knew there was no turning back.

From this point forward, Robert the Bruce would lead a renewed rebellion against England and stand as a freedom fighter for the Scottish people. Robert the Bruce gathered an army and began waging war against English positions in Scotland. His first target was Dumfries Castle, which he managed to take over without a fight when he and his men intimidated the English guards into surrendering outright.

Robert the Bruce then attempted to tie up loose ends on the ideological front by meeting up with Robert Wishart, a bishop in Glasgow. Robert the Bruce feared excommunication for the killing of John Comyn and sought reassurance from the bishop that this would not be the case. Bishop Wishart was indeed sympathetic and personally attempted to absolve Bruce of any wrongdoing as it pertained to Comyn.

But it would not be that easy for Robert the Bruce to wash John Comyn's blood away. In time, the pope would indeed excommunicate Robert the Bruce from the Catholic Church for his actions. But for the moment, the word of Bishop Wishart was enough for the Scottish, and despite the murder of John Comyn, Robert the Bruce was hailed as the new Scottish king on March 25th, 1306, in the ancestrally important Scottish town of Scone.

Once Robert the Bruce was given the crown, he was instantly at war with England, as the country no longer recognized Scotland to have any such right. Upon hearing of what had happened, Edward is said to have been frustrated and infuriated. He had just spent an enormous amount of blood and treasure to put down the Scottish revolt and was ready to finally put the matter to rest, but Robert the Bruce, of all people, had to disrupt the whole thing.

Since Bruce had been so compliant in the past, King Edward considered him pacified and was not expecting such tidings. Edward was so taken aback by the whole thing that he was initially unsure of what to do. He was quite dumbfounded. As the Scottish chronicler and poet John Barbour later described it, "And when bold Edward was told how Bruce, who was so bold, had finished off the Comyn, and then made himself king, he went nearly out of his mind."

The events were so shocking that it is generally believed they contributed to a sudden decline in Edward's health. The king was quite busy and active in the first few weeks of 1306, but after hearing of this event, which occurred in late March, he seems to have almost shut down completely. Rather than taking action, he became idle and hunkered down in Winchester as if in a stupor. When he finally left Winchester that May, he did not even walk under his own power—the old king was actually transported on a litter.

At this point, Edward seemed to understand that his strength had left him. Yet, he still knew he had to have Robert the Bruce's rebellion stopped. He turned to younger men to lead his military, appointing notable veterans such as Baron Henry Percy and Aymer de Valence, 2nd Earl of Pembroke. He also had his son, Edward II, once again lead an army of his own.

Valence made the first major moves, reaching Glasgow that June and occupying Perth on June 18th. He then moved his troops over to Methven, where he was able to intercept Bruce's roving warriors early in the morning. Bruce only had a few hundred troops at his disposal, and his small band was dwarfed by the massive English army sent to subdue it. However, Bruce's men were more used to the rough terrain, and as the English stumbled, the Scottish were able to vigorously keep their opponents at bay long enough to escape. Bruce survived to see another day.

Nevertheless, Bruce did not have the time to properly safeguard his own family, and they would ultimately be targeted by the English as a cruel means of getting at him. Robert the Bruce had a little help from his brother Neil, who managed to shepherd Bruce's wife and daughters to Kildrummy Castle in Aberdeenshire. It was not long before the English tracked Neil's movements and laid siege to Kildrummy.

Upon overrunning the fortress, they took Bruce's wife and daughters into custody, knowing they would be valuable bargaining chips as hostages. Neil was also seized, but there was no intention of sparing his life. He was promptly tried and executed on charges of treason. There were pleas from others to spare Neil, but Edward paid them no heed. He further showed his contempt by punishing the women who were captured by putting them in cages. They were otherwise left unharmed and were cared for, but the humiliation of being put on display in a cage for all to see, like some beast of burden, must have been unbearable.

The sheer lengths that the elder Edward was willing to go to in order to punish his enemies must have made some question his sanity. Even the English were not completely spared Edward's wrath. On one occasion, a group of English nobles tasked with rooting out supporters of Robert the Bruce had suddenly given up the search and decided to engage in sport among themselves instead. Edward heard of their shenanigans and had them arrested. Edward was further enraged to find out that many of these knights who found it more prudent to joust and play with each other than follow the king's orders were associates of his son Edward II. The crown prince had, as of late, been seriously grating the elder king's nerves. And it seems that even Edward's own son was not immune to his rancor.

At one point, Edward I is said to have physically assaulted his own son. Edward had learned that his son had sought to give a valuable estate to a friend of his, Piers Gaveston. King Edward summoned his son and asked about the matter. After Edward II confirmed his intention to have Piers be given the estate, the king erupted in fury.

King Edward shouted, "You bastard son of a bitch! Now you want to give lands away—you who never gained any? As the Lord lives, were it not for fear of breaking up the kingdom, you should never enjoy your inheritance!" He then grabbed hold of his son's head and tore clumps of his hair out. Edward II, no doubt, could have stood up to his father if he dared but was seemingly too afraid to do so.

After all, his father held all of the cards. And the king could cut Edward II out of his inheritance if he so desired. Edward I had worked hard to establish his kingdom, and he felt his son was simply giving it all away. The very thought of losing even a small portion of the realm he had amassed filled Edward with a great and terrible rage. Edward's contemporaries would indeed look back on the events during his final retribution against the Scottish as a veritable "reign of terror."

Chapter 11 – King Edward's Last Days

"Death has taken him, alas!"

-Peter Langtoft

King Edward was frustrated with the progress of the latest war with Scotland from the outset, and when word arrived of his force's first official defeat by Robert the Bruce in April 1307, he was absolutely appalled. His commanders were quite nervous given all of Edward's previous threats and condemnations of what he perceived to be a lackadaisical approach to crushing the revolt. As such, they seem to have rushed themselves to the point of being completely unprepared when they finally tracked down Bruce and his army in the vicinity of Glen Trool in the vast hilly terrain of Galloway, Scotland.

Whatever the case may be, the English troops were apparently not ready. Even though Bruce fielded a smaller force, the Scottish troops were able to strike back hard enough against the English to force them to retreat. In truth, much credit should probably be given to Robert the Bruce's ingenious military tactics. Bruce had men strategically stationed on the high ground surrounding the glen. As soon as the English approached, he signaled them with a bugle call. The men then began rolling huge stones down on top of the English.

The English troops were not ready for this, and in the midst of their confusion, Bruce took the initiative and signaled his troops to charge. The sheer audacity of this onslaught managed to push the English back. The stunned English fought a successful rearguard action, keeping causalities to a minimum, but the mere fact they were forced to flee was an unbearable humiliation to King Edward.

Here he was, spending precious money and resources to crush another revolt, and it seemed as if his incompetent commanders were squandering it all. Edward was a man of action and likely desired to be at the front lines directing the battles himself, but due to his deteriorating health, he was not able to do so.

Even more alarming things were to come. The following month, on May 10th, Aymer de Valence's forces were soundly defeated at Loudon Hill.

Bruce employed yet another ingenious strategy during this engagement by digging trenches all around Loudon Hill and then concealing pikemen inside of them. Trench warfare wouldn't exactly come into vogue until World War One, yet here Robert the Bruce was, utilizing it several centuries prior. And the English army simply was not expecting men with long pikes to be hiding underground.

So, when the English charged across the plains and headed toward Loudon Hill, it was easy for the skilled pikemen to simply rise up and stab and slash the Englishmen and their horses as they passed over. Valence's army was absolutely decimated. Robert the Bruce's strategies were so ingenious and thought-provoking that they have given rise to an intriguing yet completely theoretical explanation for the reason behind Bruce's military acumen.

The same year these events were taking place in Scotland, a certain group of elite fighters known as the Knights Templar was being persecuted by the king of France. They had been accused of trumped-up charges of heresy. Their compound would be raided, and their leader, Jacques de Molay, would be arrested and later burned at the stake. Several high-ranking Templars would be thrown in prison. Some likely saw the writing on the wall and left France before it was too late.

It has been theorized that some Templars may have even made their way to Scotland. Thus, it has been suggested that wandering Templars might have actually hooked up with Robert the Bruce during that fateful year of 1307. Could it be that the Knights Templar were helping to direct and train Robert the Bruce's Scottish resistance against the English? Again, this is all theoretical speculation that has never been proven, but it certainly is a thought-provoking idea to entertain.

Robert the Bruce followed up his stunning victory at Loudon Hill by heading north to take the strategic fortresses of Inverlochy and Urquhart. He then subsequently razed two other castles—Inverness and Nairn—leaving nothing but a pile of smoking rubble behind. King Edward was growing understandably alarmed at these developments, and the stress of these embarrassing defeats may very well have hastened his decline. Edward was now certain that if the war was going to be won, he would have to lead it himself.

He set in motion plans to build a large contingent of troops around the town of Carlisle that would be ready for him to take charge of by July. Right when the king was getting ready to make good on his intentions, he began to be plagued with a severe bout of dysentery. His physicians attempted to use the best medicine at their disposal, which largely consisted of the application of various ointments and tinctures, but none of it seemed to help.

Despite their best efforts, the sixty-eight-year-old king seemed to be getting worse. Due to his sickness, he was largely immobile for several days at a time, leading some to speculate the king was dying. But then, by sheer force of will, Edward got himself out of bed and insisted he would make the trip out to Carlisle to lead the troops. But besides a few steps from his bedside, he could not walk. So, again, the king was put inside a litter that would be carried to his destination. This was disposed of at Carlisle Cathedral, where Edward was carefully placed on a horse.

The tired and deathly sick king clutched the steed for dear life. He was attempting to demonstrate that he still had it in him to lead the troops. However, the king would not make it far, and after a journey of just six miles, he could go no farther. Edward was taken off his horse on July 6th, 1307, and the sick king was laid to rest at a makeshift camp.

The next day, on July 7th, Edward was roused by his servants in an attempt to feed the king lunch. They struggled to sit the sick king up to eat, but as they did so, the king's weary lungs took in one last gasp of air before breathing no more. It has been said that King Edward fell limp and passed away right there on the spot. Despite his desire to finish the business in Scotland, this battle was destined to be finished by someone else.

Conclusion: The Hammer of the Scots and Lessons Learned

The death of any wartime leader can be a troublesome prospect. Even in the United States, a nation in which the succession of leadership is carefully assured by way of official protocol could be troubling, especially if it occurred during a period of war. President Franklin Delano Roosevelt, for example, abruptly passed at the tail end of World War Two, provoking great anxiety over the swearing-in of his vice president, Harry S. Truman. Yes, as it pertains to major wars, most would generally like to see the leaders who were present at the start of them be there for the conclusion.

And in King Edward's England, this was most certainly the case. In England, the idea that the English monarch had perished, even with Crown Prince Edward II ready to take over, was perceived as a tremendous vulnerability. So much so that in the first few weeks of Edward I's passing, the situation was basically treated as a confidential state secret. It has been said that if anyone in the king's inner circle even so much as mentioned it, they could have been thrown in prison.

The last thing the English needed was for their enemies to detect weakness, so the news of King Edward's passing was initially kept as quiet as possible. These few weeks of secrecy were deemed crucial for the transfer of power to Edward II. Even though his father died on July 7th, Edward II would not be officially announced until July 20th. It was only then the people of England were let in on the fact that their long-lived monarch, Edward I, was no more.

King Edward II held elaborate ceremonies for his father before he rushed off to oversee the war effort in Scotland. Since Edward II inherited his father's crown, he also inherited his father's war.

In the early years of Edward II's reign, Robert the Bruce seemed to hold the upper hand, and in 1310, he attempted to capitalize on this fact by offering the new king a truce. Edward II was just as stubborn as his father, and he refused to entertain the notion. Edward II would actually continue fighting the resurgent Scottish for the rest of his life. By the time of his passing in 1327, the war still raged. When his son, Edward III, took the reins of power, a peace agreement between England and Scotland would finally be made.

One must wonder what King Edward I would have thought about what happened after his death. King Edward had sought a quick and decisive victory against Scotland. The "Hammer of the Scots" wanted to hammer Scotland into submission.

Yet such a thing ultimately proved impossible for him and his immediate descendants to achieve. The nation of Scotland, which Edward had once flippantly referred to as nothing more than a "turd," proved that it was willing to stand up to English oppression at all costs. It may have taken a total of three King Edwards to learn this lesson, but it was indeed a valuable one.

Here's another book by Captivating History that you might like

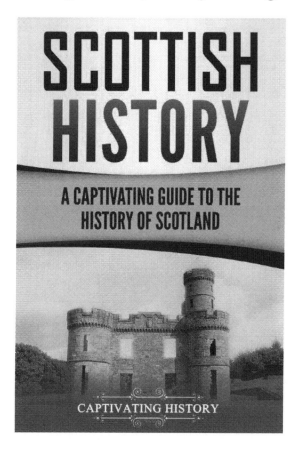

Free Bonus from Captivating History (Available for a Limited time)

Hi History Lovers!

Now you have a chance to join our exclusive history list so you can get your first history ebook for free as well as discounts and a potential to get more history books for free! Simply visit the link below to join.

Captivatinghistory.com/ebook

Also, make sure to follow us on Facebook, Twitter and Youtube by searching for Captivating History.

Appendix A: Further Reading and Reference

A Great and Terrible King: Edward I and the Forging of Britain. Marc Morris. 2008.

William Wallace: Brave Heart. James Mackay. 1995.